**COLLECTOR'S PRICE GUIDE**

# WESTERN MOVIE

## PHOTOGRAPHS AND AUTOGRAPHS

### 50 YEARS OF WESTERN MOVIES 1920'S-1970'S

**Ken Owens**

*Schiffer Publishing Ltd*

4880 Lower Valley Road Atglen, Pennsylvania 19310

**Other Schiffer Books on Related Subjects:**
*Cowboy Collectibles and Western Memorabilia.* Bob Ball & Edward Vebell. ISBN: 0887405053. $29.95
*Stetson Hats & the John B. Stetson Company: 1865-1970.* Jeffrey B. Snyder. ISBN: 0764302116. $39.95
*Western Memorabilia and Collectibles.* Bob Ball. ISBN: 0887404847. $19.95

Type set in Frutiger LT Std/Times New Roman

ISBN: 978-0-7643-3934-9
Printed in China

Schiffer Books are available at special discounts for bulk purchases for sales promotions or premiums. Special editions, including personalized covers, corporate imprints, and excerpts can be created in large quantities for special needs. For more information contact the publisher:

Published by Schiffer Publishing Ltd.
4880 Lower Valley Road
Atglen, PA 19310
Phone: (610) 593-1777; Fax: (610) 593-2002
E-mail: Info@schifferbooks.com

For the largest selection of fine reference books on this and related subjects, please visit our website at **www.schifferbooks.com**
We are always looking for people to write books on new and related subjects. If you have an idea for a book, please contact us at proposals@schifferbooks.com

This book may be purchased from the publisher.
Include $5.00 for shipping.
Please try your bookstore first.
You may write for a free catalog.

In Europe, Schiffer books are distributed by
Bushwood Books
6 Marksbury Ave.
Kew Gardens
Surrey TW9 4JF England
Phone: 44 (0) 20 8392 8585; Fax: 44 (0) 20 8392 9876
E-mail: info@bushwoodbooks.co.uk
Website: www.bushwoodbooks.co.uk

# Contents

# Preface

This preface shows the part of the American Indian in American history, in general, and the Indian's particular role in western movie history. For our immediate history, the Indian has been a part of it since the 1600s and the American cowboy since the mid-1800s. The Indian's ancestors date back 20,000 years. Cowboys post-date the American Civil War.

One of the few bad marks against western movies is the Indians have been portrayed as savages attacking white settlers and pioneers in their quest for "Manifest Destiny."

This is partially true because, in the Indian culture, they attacked each other for sport as much as battle, to get horses, slaves, food, or to show bravery by counting coup.

Over the years, for real and in movies, attitudes have been, as Mel Gibson said in *Maverick*, "It's the Indian's fault for living on our land before we got here."

Later movie makers have tried to change that image. Even John Ford felt bad for his treatment of the Indians. He tried to make it up in *Cheyenne Autumn*. But, probably because of the lack of Indian actors, he still used Spanish actors in Indian roles.

The best efforts in recent years to portray Indians in a truthful light were: Delmer Daves' *Broken Arrow*, with Jimmy Stewart, Jeff Chandler, and Debra Paget; Richard Harris in *A Man Called Horse*; and Kevin Costner's *Dances with Wolves*.

It appears everyone gets their due sooner or later.

Indians were self-sufficient when the country was theirs. They lived off nature, neither spoiling, wasting or changing it. They adjusted to their environment and lived within its limits. Their traditions and religions were strong. Some had very high cultures that included arts, crafts, architecture, irrigation farming, entertainment, and sports. They were able to govern themselves and run their own affairs, whether they lived in a group of five families or a community of thousands of people. From the 1860-65 Civil War and Quantrill's Raiders, there existed a lineage of western outlaws through the 1920s depression. They all roamed the Cookson Hills of eastern Oklahoma. They were the James Gang, the Younger Brothers, the Daltons, Bill Doolin gang, and Pretty Boy Floyd. At least one or more members from each gang went on to the next, seemingly an inherited quality.

Oklahoma, being Indian territory until 1909, was a safe haven for outlaws like the above when running from the law. The lawmen who worked out of Judge Parker's court in Fort Smith, Arkansas, included the four guardsmen: Heck Thomas, Chris Madsen, Bill Tilghman, and E. D. Nix, along with others.

The 1880s cowtowns grew up in Kansas, receiving cattle drives from Texas. This brought about other lawmen like Wild Bill Hickok, Wyatt Earp, Bat Masterson, and Pat Garrett.

All these histories, the Indian's, outlaw's and lawmen's, and the history of the cowboy, together were brought into focus by Buffalo Bill and other Wild West shows and the dime novels like Ned Buntline's. These colorful histories, shows, and novels made perfect fodder for the motion picture industry, and especially the birth and development of the westerns. Look for photos of these historical figures near the end of the book.

# Foreword

There is nothing like the American West, its splendor, its grandeur, expanse of wide skies, majestic mountains, flowing streams, air to breath, and hopefully the vision to see, feel, and live the vastness of it all. Together, these characteristics become the reason for most of the interest in the American West, and the western movies.

The western movie has been the most popular type of film since its beginning over 100 years ago. The Greeks had mythological heroes, England had its Camelot and Robin Hood, and America had its cowboys.

The cowboy stands for freedom and his environment is vast desert plains, rugged mountains, and free-flowing streams, with only a few settlers and Indians. They went where they wanted, their freedom of action contrasting with most people's lives today.

Physical toughness, self-reliance, sincerity, and basic masculinity of the cowboy still appeals to us today. The western hero's courage was balanced by his modesty. His physical violence was balanced by a reluctance to use force. Only when there was no other way did he use his six-shooter.

Thomas A. Edison, inventor of the motion picture camera of course, used western themes. No plots, just one minute vignette film reels shown in arcades on kinetoscopes or peep-show machines.

Not only were there real cowboys and Indians, but real lawmen and outlaws at that time. The popularity of Buffalo Bill's Wild West Show and Ned Buntline's "dime novels" helped the western's popularity in this new medium of filmmaking (movies), as mentioned in the Preface.

These peep-shows became western stories and ran a full ten minutes. The plot set the formula for westerns for years to come.

Broncho Billy Anderson became the first cowboy hero in western movies and the ancestor to "B" westerns. James Cruze's *The Covered Wagon* (1923) and John Ford's *The Iron Horse* (1924) became the first epic westerns, lasting up to two hours.

# Dedication

This book is dedicated to the luminaries who had the interest and foresight to invent films, and especially the westerns. These include Thomas Edison, and his early projection system, Edwin S. Porter, D. W. Griffith, Thomas Ince, and others who developed the system for making and showing movies. They include the early playwrights, cinematographers, and directors like John Ford.

Also included are the earliest of western actors, like Broncho Billy Anderson and Francis Ford, with others following like William S. Hart, Harry Carey, Tom Mix, Buck Jones, and all the rest.

Finally, let's not forget the public who attended, for whatever reason, from the earliest western motion picture until today's efforts.

Thomas Edison

Broncho Billy
rediscovered
50 years later

Thomas Ince

Cecil B. DeMille

# Introduction

This book includes about 2,000 western movie star photos and signatures, with each identified and priced. These photos depict stars starting with the 1920s silent films and moving forward to the 1970s films. When "talkies" first became a part of western movies in 1928, many thought the western was through, but the films just got better.

Most of the photographs shown include autographs. For those that do not, they are identified and the value of those actors' signatures are provided.

Each signature's value will be estimated: signed letters – worth the most; signed photos – second; and clip signatures – worth the least. Ordinary, unsigned picture values in the book are covered on this page below:

| | | |
|---|---|---|
| Reproduction black and white | 8 x 10 | $3.00 - $5.00 |
| Reproduction color | 8 x 10 | $8.00 - $10.00 |
| Vintage photos | 8 x 10 | $30.00 - $40.00 |
| Studio photo (promo/friend) | 11 x 14 | $30.00 - $40.00 |

All photos, letters, and clip signatures are valued based on age, size, condition of photo, signature, and the author's 50 years of experience in collecting.

This book is mainly created to allow the reader to visualize the actor and to recognize the signature. It is also written for you to enjoy, and hopefully to create new interest in the western genre, and revive old interests. Like I said, *my* interest has been constant for over 60 years.

The western movie saved the entire movie industry several times in the past. New film makers need to remember that.

— Ken Owens, author

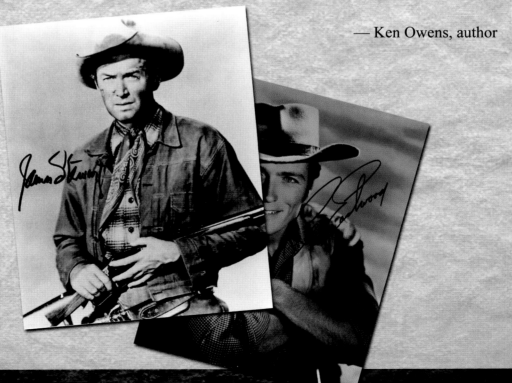

# 50 Years of Western Movies

# Chapter One
## 1920s - Silent Westerns

# G.M. "Broncho Billy" Anderson
## 1880-1971

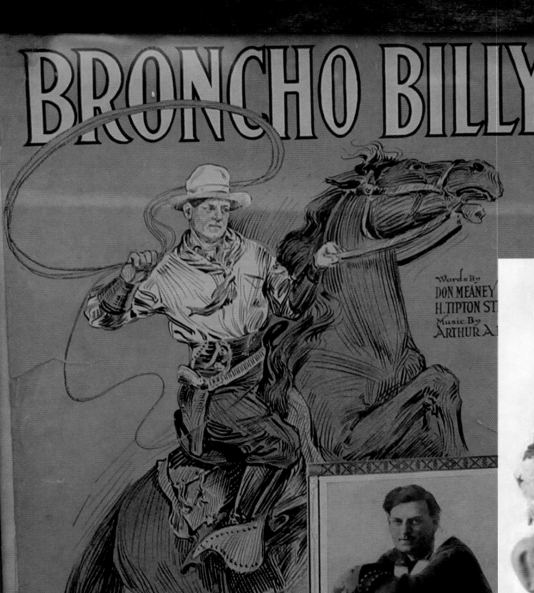

America's first cowboy movie star,
Broncho Billy Anderson AKA Max Aaronson.
Autograph Estimated Value - $800.00 - $1,000.00

With Francis X. Bushman
and Charlie Chaplin.

**Autographed Picture - Estimated Value - $800.00 - $1000.00**

WILLIAM FOX
*Presents*
DUSTIN FARNUM
*in*
IRON TO GOLD

rgue with
Dealer
man himself

Dustin Farnum
"The Squaw Man"

13

# William Farnum 1876-1953

**Autographed Picture** **Estimated Value - $300.00 - $500.00**

WILLIAM FARNUM

Autographed Picture - Estimated Value - $400.00 - $600.00

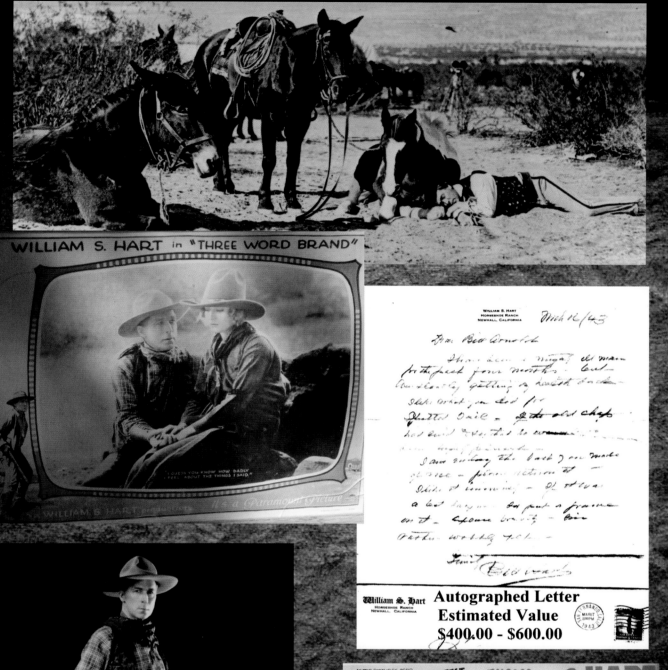

WILLIAM S. HART in "THREE WORD BRAND"

Autographed Letter
Estimated Value
$400.00 - $600.00

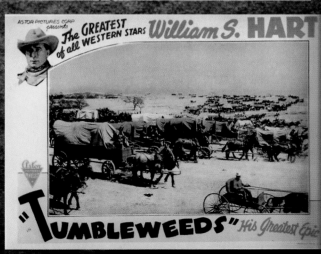

Lobby Card - Estimated Value - $100.00 - $150.00

# Harry Carey Sr. 1878-1947

Autographed Picture - Estimated Value - $400.00 - $600.00

With George Hayes and Julian Rivero.

**Autographed Picture - Estimated Value - $300.00 - $500.00**

**Autographed Picture - Estimated Value - $700.00 - $900.00**

**Autographed Photo - Estimated Value - $700.00 - $900.00**

# Tom Mix

Greetings from
Tom and Tony Jr.

**$400.00 - $600.00**

AFTER FIVE DAYS RETURN TO

**MARSHALL FIELD & COMPANY**

ADAMS, QUINCY, FRANKLIN AND WELLS

CHICAGO, ILL.

CHICAGO
MAR 7
3 00PM
1925
ILL.

## Clip Signature
## $300.00 - $500.00

TOM MIX PRODUCTIONS

PERSONAL
CORRESPONDENCE

May 26th, 1928.

Miss Florence Ulrich,
Gregg Publishing Co.,
20 West 47th Street,
New York City.

My dear Miss Ulrich:

I wish to acknowledge
your letter of recent date and thank you
very much for same.   I am indeed happy to
learn that I pleased you to such an extent.

With reference to a photo-
graph I would advise that you mail your request
c/o Tom Mix, F. B. O. Studios, Hollywood, California.

Yours very truly,

TOM MIX.

TOM MIX PRODUCTIONS

## Lobby Card

## Letter Signature
## $700.00 - $900.00

Blue Belle Saloon-Guthrie, Okla.

**Tom Mix Gravesite**
**Florence, Arizona**

**Fox Stars**
**1930's - 1940's**

# Buck Jones    1889/91-1942

**Autographed Photo - Estimated Value - $500.00 - $700.00**

To My Pal, Roy Mac Lean
Here's stinkens at you
Buck Jones

**Autographed Photos -Signed to Roy Mac Lean, Fox Photographer**
**Estimated Value - $900.00 - $1100.00 (for both)**

# Buck Jones (Rough Riders)

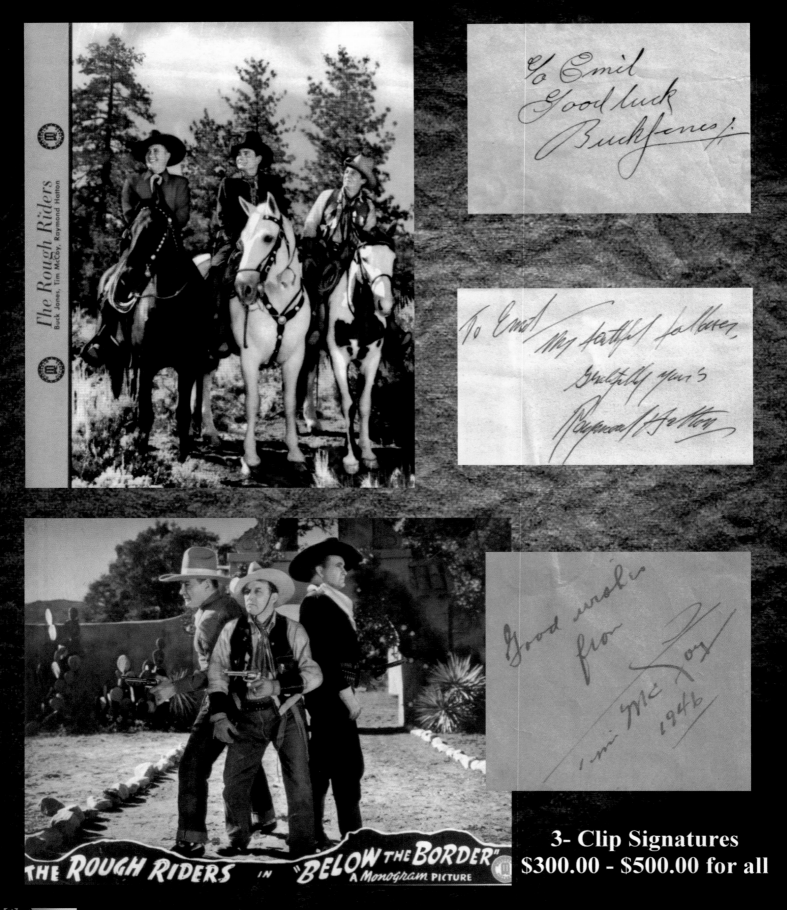

**Buck Jones & Family Signed by Wife & Daughter $200.00 - $300.00**

# Ken Maynard 1895-1973

To "Bertha"
A great little girl"
Ken Maynard 1937.

- SAHLI -
APPLETON WIS
1937 ©

**Autographed Picture - Estimated Value - $600.00 - $800.00**

To [...] Ken Maynard 1952

To our good old Time friends Floyd & Florence—May our Trails Cross often. 1956 Ken & Bertha Maynard

Sincere To "Marguerite" Stanton Ken Maynard 1946

2- Ken Maynard Lobby Cards - $50.00 ea.

# Hoot Gibson 1892-1962

**Autographed Photo to Jack Hoxie signed 'Hoot' -$400.00 - $600.00**

Hoot Gibson in an early pose.

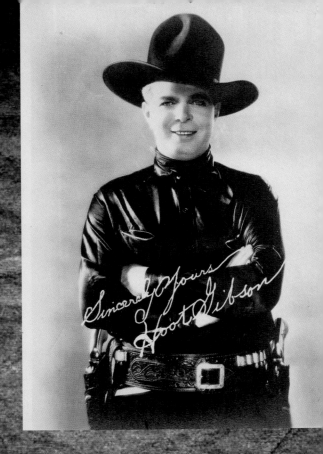

Sincerely Yours
Hoot Gibson

M.H. HOFFMAN Jr.
PRESENTS

Hoot Gibson

THE
FIGHTING
PARSON

WITH
MARCELINE DAY
ROBERT FRAZER
STANLEY BLYSTONE
skeeter BILL ROBBINS
directed by HARRY FRAZER

Best

Hoot Gibson

Clip Signature   $200.00   $300.0

# Tim McCoy 1891-1978

**Autographed Photo- Estimated Value -$400.00 - $600.00**

# Jack Holt  1888-1951

**Autographed Photo- Estimated Value -$400.00 - $600.00**

# eorge O'Brien   1899-1985

**Autographed Photo- Estimated Value - $400.00 - $600.00**

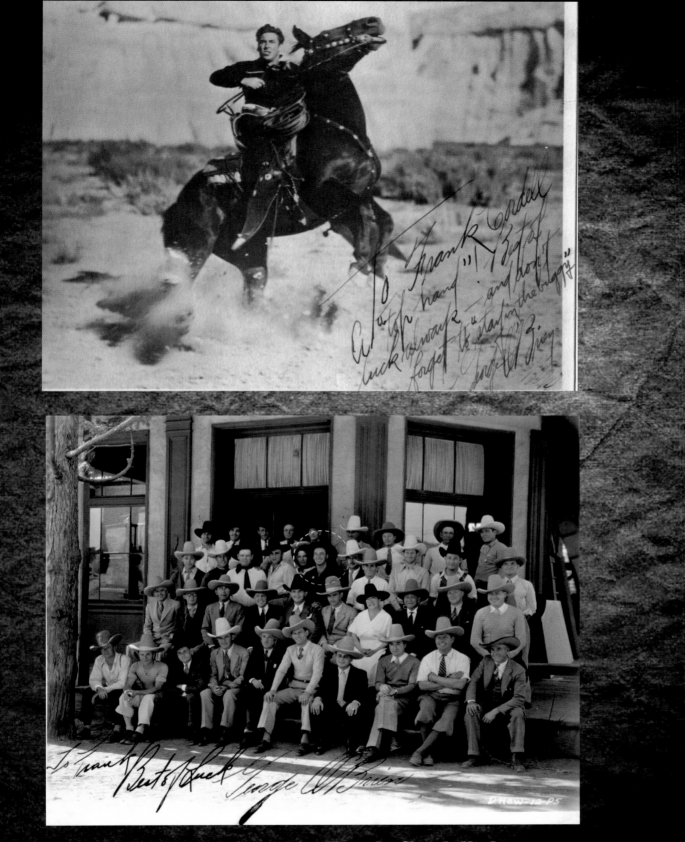

**Both photos signed to Frank Cordell shown
to the right of O'Brien in the group photo.
Estimated value $600.00 - $800.00 for both.**

# GEORGE O'BRIEN
# HOLLYWOOD COWBOY

Lobby Card- Estimated Value -$40.00 - $60.00

BULLET CODE
An RKO Radio Picture

49/377

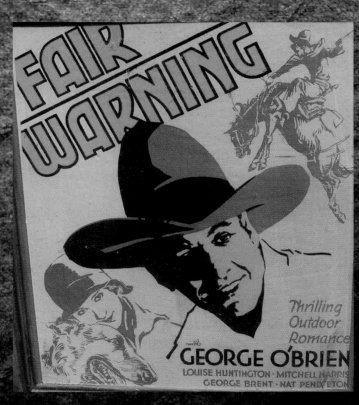

**Autographed photo**
**Estimated value $200.00 - $300.00**

**Poster**
**Estimated value $100.00 - $200.00**

# Fred Thomson 1890-1928

**Autographed Photo- Estimated Value -$800.00 - $1000.00**

Large Poster
Estimated value $300.00 - $400.00

Lobby Card
Estimated value $100.00 - $200.00

# Richard Dix 1893-1949

**Autographed Photo
Estimated Value
$400.00 - $600.00**

*"Cimmaron"*

*"The Vanishing American"*   **Clip Signature - $100.00 - $200.00**

# Warner Baxter
## 1889-1951

Warner Baxter.

**Autographed Photo**
**Estimated Value**
**$300.00 - $500.00**

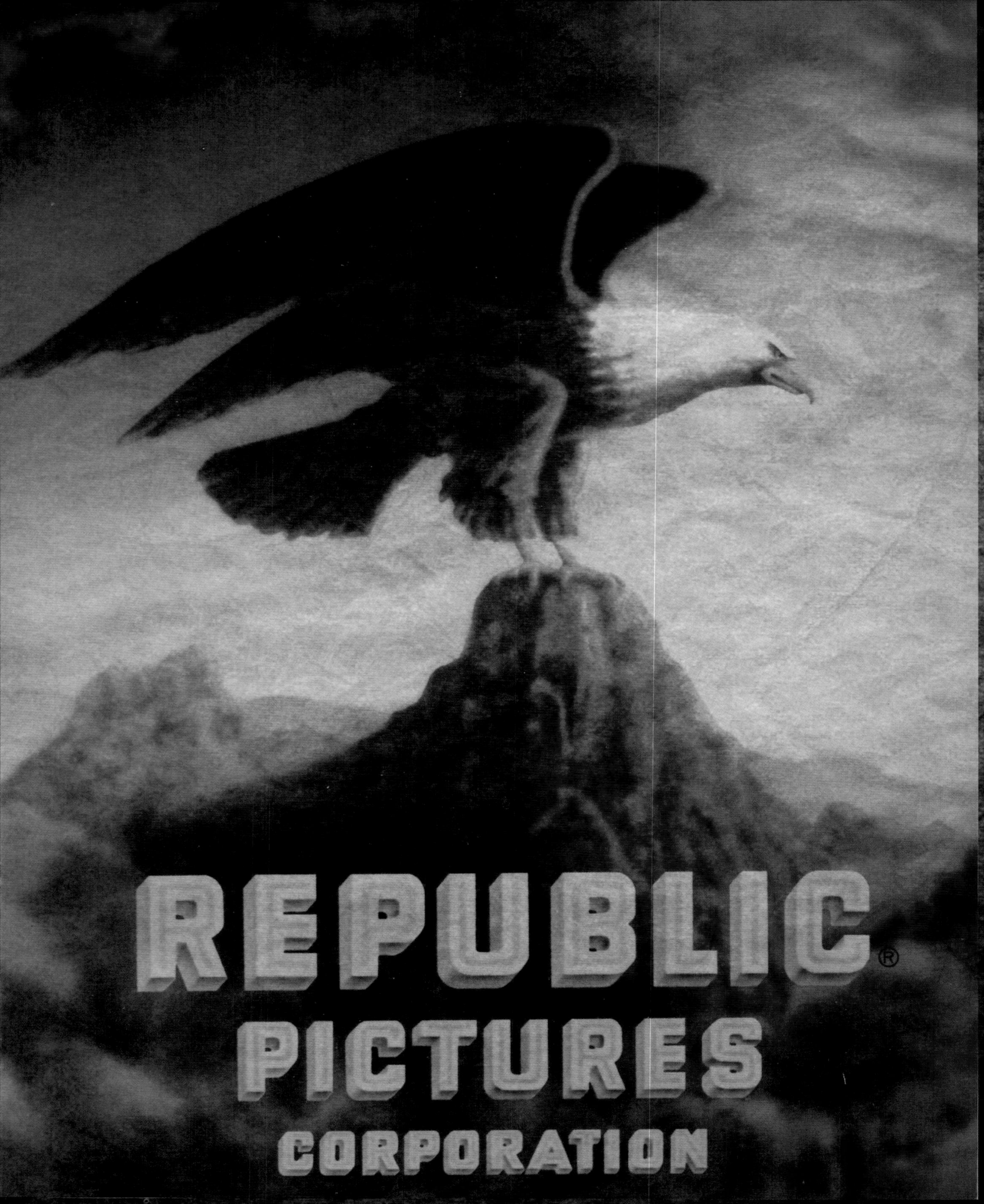
REPUBLIC®
PICTURES
CORPORATION

# Chapter Two
## 1930's - Early 'B' Westerns

# Jack Hoxie 1885-1965

*For Greater Movie Season* Jack Hoxie

**Autographed Photo - Estimated Value -$200.00 - $300.00**

# Al Hoxie   1901-1982

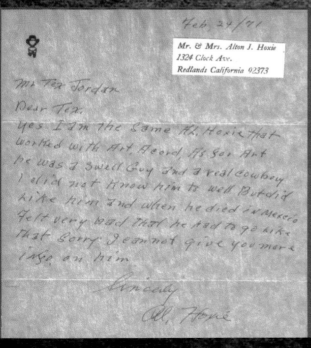

**Autographed Photo - Estimated Value -$200.00 - $300.00**
**Signed Letter - Estimated Value - $300.00 - $400.00**
**Clip Signature - Estimated Value -$200.00 - $300.00**

# Art Acord
## 1890-1931

With Esther Ralston
in *"Gypsy Trail"*
(1918 Paramount)

**Autograph Not Shown - Estimated Value Signed - $200.00 - $300.00**

# Buddy Roosevelt 1898-1973

WILL'S
Three Castles
"Vice Regal"
CIGARETTES

PETE MORRISON
(UNIVERSAL)

Autographed Photo - Estimated Value - $200.00 - $300.00
(unsigned photos shown)

# ob Livingston 1904-1988

**Autographed Photo - Estimated Value - $400.00 - $600.00**

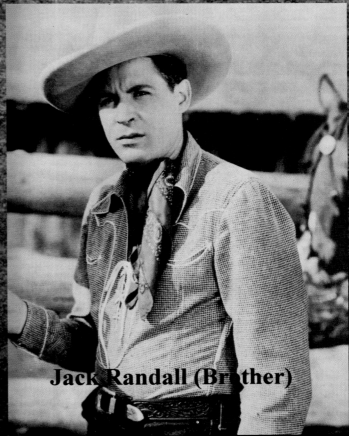

Jack Randall (Brother)

Autographed Photo (11X14) - Estimated Value - $400.00 - $600.00

# Tom Tyler    1903-1954

**Autographed Photo - Estimated Value - $300.00 - $500.00**

54

"Greetings" from Tom Tyler

# Tom Keene 1896-1963

**Clip Signature - Estimated Value - $100.00 - $200.00**
**Autographed Photos - Estimated Value Signed - $200.00 - $400.00**

# Dave "Tex" O'Brien   1912-1969

With Tex Ritter and Guy Wilkerson.

With I. Stanford Jolley

THE RANGERS TAKE OVER

DAVE (TEX) O'BRIEN and NEWILL —The Texas Rangers

Jim Newill   1911-1935

PRODUCERS RELEASING CORPORATION presents "SHOOTIN' IRONS" with DAVE (TEX) O'BRIEN and JIM NEWILL

**Autograph Not Shown - Estimated Value Signed - $100.00 - $200.00**

# William Desmond  1872-1922

# Edmund Cobb  1892-1974

**Autographed Photos - Estimated Value - $100.00 - $200.00**

# Rex Bell 1903-1962

With my best
Wishes
Rex Bell

**Autographed photo - Estimated Value - $300.00 - $500.00**

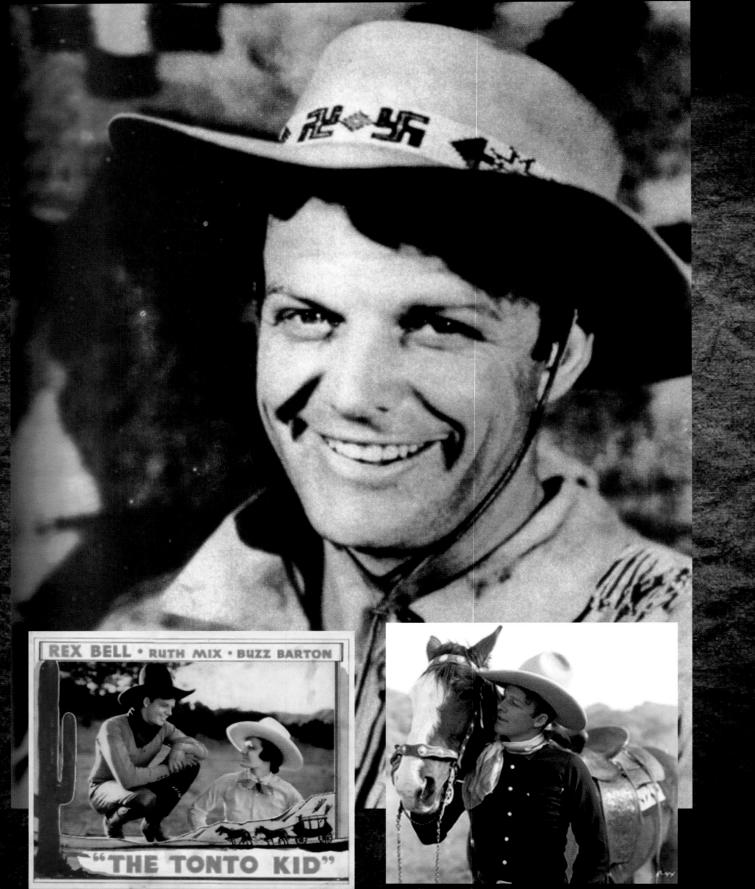

REX BELL • RUTH MIX • BUZZ BARTON

"THE TONTO KID"

# hn "Dusty" King 1909-1987

**Autographed photo - Estimated Value - $200.00 - $300.00**

# Jack Luden 1902-1951

Autographed photo - Estimated Value - $100.00 - $200.00

# George Houston 1896-1944

GEORGE HOUSTON- Metro Goldwyn-Mayer

Producers Releasing Corp. presents GEORGE HOUSTON in, "THE LONE RIDER FIGHTS BACK."   Printed in U.S.A.

GH-73-19

Autograph Not Shown - Estimated Value Signed - $100.00 - $200.00

# Bob Custer & Jack Perrin

Jack Perrin
1896-1967

Leo Maloney

Wally
Wales

Bob Custer
1898-1974

Buffalo Bill Jr.

Autographed photo - Estimated Value - $100.00 - $300.00

# Bob "Tex" Allen   1906-1998

Bob Allen

**Autographed photo - Estimated Value -  $200.00 - $400.00**

# Ray "Crash" Corrigan
### 1902-1976

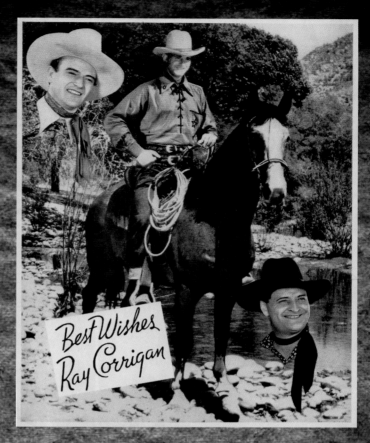

Best Wishes
Ray Corrigan

**With Rita Cansino later Rita Hayworth**

**RAY CORRIGAN**

**Autographed Photo - Estimated Value - $300.00 - $500.00**

William Colt MacDonald's Three Mesquiteer movie *"Powersmoke Range"* (1935) fostered other Three Mesquiteer movies and prolonged fading careers of other actors by teaming them as trios in such movies as *"Rough Rider,"* *"Range Busters,"* and *"Trial Blazers."*

*"The Three Mesquiteers:"* 1 with Bob Livingston, 2 with John Wayne, Crash Corrigan, and Max Terhune.

with Duncan Renaldo and ... *"Rough Riders:"* with Buck Jones, Tim McCoy, and

with Chief Thundercloud.

## *"Trailblazers"*
with Hoot Gibson, Bob Steele and Rocky Cameron, and later joined by Ken Maynard.

## *"Rangebusters"*
and other trios ending in 1943.

with Dennis Moore.

Guy Wilkerson, Dave O'Brien and Jim Newall.

with Raymond Hattom and heavies Jack Ingram and LeRoy Mason.

with Dave Sharpe and John Dusty King.

# Chapter Three
## 1940's - Later 'B' Westerns

# Johnny Mack Brown 1904-1974

**Autographed photo - Estimated Value - $400.00 - $500.00**

STATEMENT

Artist's Name: JOHNNY MACK BROWN

Title of Picture: "WEST OF WYOMING"

Character or Role: STAR

Type of Contract: TERM

Disputed Claim

Amount originally paid for services in picture: $~~1,280.00~~

Amount due @ 12½% of original payment: $~~173.08~~ $100.00

RELEASE

For and in consideration of the payment to the undersigned of the sum of $173.08 , computed as set forth in the above statement, receipt of which sum is hereby acknowledged by the undersigned, the undersigned hereby releases Monogram Pictures Corporation, Monogram Productions, Inc., Allied Artists Pictures Corp., Allied Artists Productions, Inc., and their respective officers, agents, employees, affiliates, subsidiaries, licensees, successors and assigns of and from any and all claims, demands and causes of action arising out of or in connection with the televising of that certain picture entitled "WEST OF WYOMING" , in accordance with and subject to the terms of that certain agreement between Monogram Pictures Corporation and Screen Actors Guild, Inc. dated May 9, 1952. Without limiting the generality of the foregoing, the undersigned hereby acknowledges and agrees that said sum shall constitute a full and complete compensation to the undersigned for the right to televise the acts, poses and appearances of the undersigned in said picture, in accordance with the terms of said agreement dated May 9, 1952. The undersigned hereby waives the benefits of the provisions of Section 1542 of the Civil Code of the State of California.

The undersigned hereby acknowledges that Monogram Pictures Corporation, Monogram Productions, Inc., Allied Artists Pictures Corp., and Allied Artists Productions, Inc., by the payment of said sum to the undersigned, do not admit that they do not own the complete rights to televise said picture, it being understood that such payment is made to compromise and settle a disputed claim.

Dated: June 18, 1956

Johny Mack Brown
JOHNNY MACK BROWN

**Signed contract - Estimated Value -  $400.00 - $600.00**

# aries Starrett (Durango Kid)
## 1903-1986

Autographed photo - Estimated Value - $300.00 - $500.00

Salud, Oliver from one who rode the Hollywood Range - Charles "Durango" Starrett

Charles STARRETT and Smiley BURNETTE in FRONTIER OUTPOST with Lois Hall, Steve Darrell, Hank Penny and Slim Duncan. Written by Barry Shipman. Directed by RAY NAZARRO. Produced by COLBERT CLARK. A COLUMBIA PICTURE

49/623

**Durango with Smiley Burnette and Jack Mahoney**
**Autographed 11X14 - $400.00 - $600.00**

# ob Steele     1907-1988

**Autographed photo - Estimated Value -  $300.00 - $500.00**

 *Bob Steele*

**Writing tablet cover**

Autographed photo - Estimated Value - $400.00 - $500.00

# Tim Holt 1919-1973

**Clip Signature - Estimated Value - $200.00 - $400.00**

**With Richard Martin.**

# Audie Murphy 1924/25-1971

**Autographed photo - Estimated Value - $500.00 - $700.00**

HE FOUGHT THE FURY OF THE APACHE WARPATH
...while his back was the target for a hundred guns!

COLOR BY TECHNICOLOR
TUMBLEWEED

Starring AUDIE MURPHY · LORI NELSON · CHILL WILLS

with K. T. STEVENS · RUSSELL JOHNSON · MADGE MEREDITH · ROY ROBERTS

**Clip Signature - Estimated Value - $400.00 - $600.00**

# Rod Cameron 1910-1983

401-75

**Clip signature - Estimated Value - $300.00 - $400.00**

ROD CAMERON

Feb. 22, 1980

Dear Jack —

Thanks for your letter inviting me to the Minneapolis Festival. August is so far away I couldn't possibly commit myself so far ahead.

It has been my experience that if I say I might attend it has been published that I'll be there. And then I get a lot of flak from people who say they went there just to see me and they resent it that I didn't show up. So I can only say that at a later date when I see how the summer is going I'll think about it.

Best
Rod Cameron

**Signed letter -  $300.00 - $500**

---

**Signed document - Estimated Value -  $400.00 - $600.00**

# Allen "Rocky" Lane 1909-1973

**Autographed photo - Estimated Value - $400.00 - $600.00**

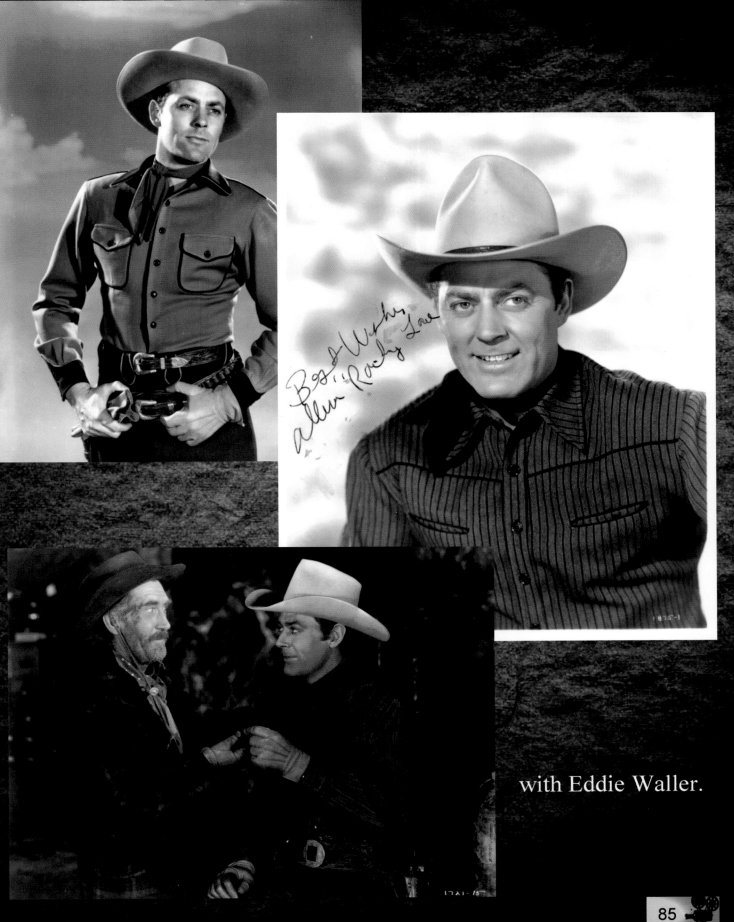

with Eddie Waller.

# on "Red" Barry 1912-1980

**Autographed photo - Estimated Value - $400.00 - $600.00**

# ster Crabbe 1908-1983

with Al "Fuzzy" St. John

utograph Not Shown - Estimated Value Signed - $200.00 - $300.00

**Autographed photo - Estimated Value - $200.00 - $300.00**

To Kier
Best Wishes
Lash LaRue
2/22/89

Whip Wilson

WMP-9-21

# unset Carson 1920-1990

**Autographed photo - Estimated Value - $200.00 - $300.00**

**With Andy Devine in**
*"The Adventures of Wild Bill Hickok"*

Guy Madison and Andy Devine

**Autographed photo - Estimated Value - $200.00 - $300.00**

SOF-107-7

# ames Ellison    1910-1993

**Autographed photo - Estimated Value - $200.00 - $300.00**

**With Russell Hayden**

# Russell Hayden 1912-1981

**Autographed photo - Estimated Value - $200.00 - $300.00**

Clip Signature
$100.00 - $200.00

**Russell Hayden and Zipper.**

# Chapter Four
## 1940's & '50's - Early 'A' Westerns

# Randolph Scott 1898-1987

**Autographed photo - Estimated Value - $400.00 - $600.00**

"Good luck!"

**Randolph Scott, Mariette Hartley, & Joel McCrea**
**Signed by all 3 - Estimated value - $800.00 - $1000,00**

A scene from "Belle Starr," one of the 50 films in 20th Century-Fox Television's FOX TWO.

Zane Grey's "THE LAST ROUND-UP" with Randolph Scott, Monte Blue, Barbara Adams and Fred Kohler
A Paramount Picture

**Autographed photo - Estimated Value - $400.00 - $600.00**

"The Virginian"

Joel McCrea with Veronica Lake, and Arlene Whelan in *"RAMROD"*

George Montgomery portrays a fightin' Mayor of CIMARRON CITY, hour-long adventure series.

mca
TV FILM SYNDICATION

# Gary Cooper
## 1901-1961

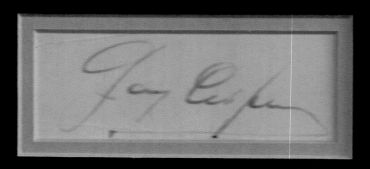

**Clip Signature - Estimated Value - $300.00 - $400.00**
**Autographed photo - Estimated Value - $700.00 - $900.00**

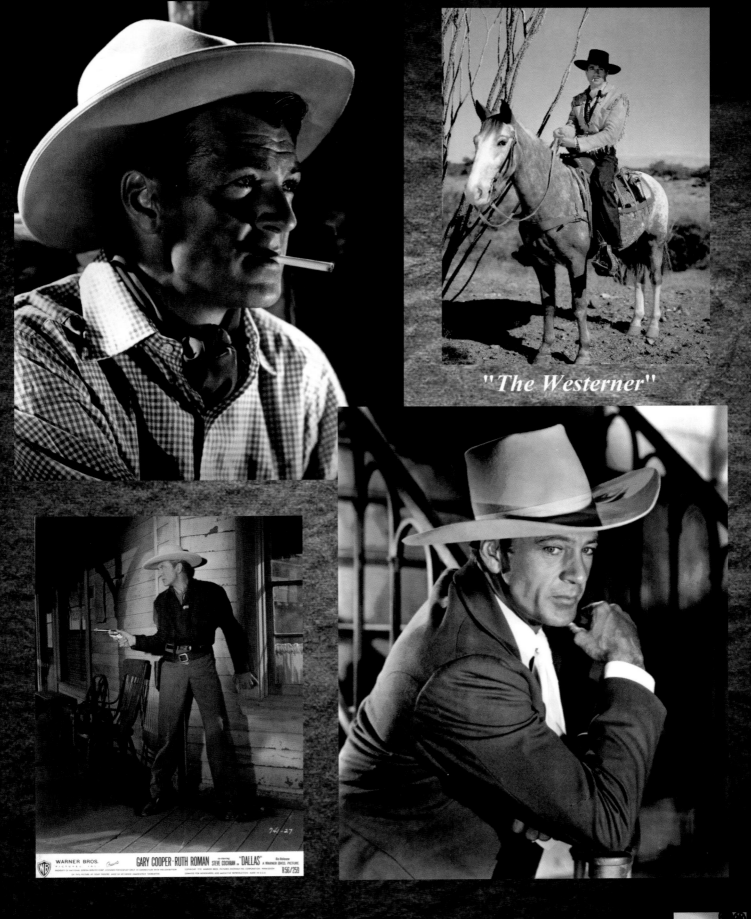

"The Westerner"

# Gary Cooper

Very truly yours
Gary Cooper
Paramount Studios

SAMUEL GOLDWYN
GARY
COOPER
MERLE
OBERON
THE
Cowboy
AND
the Lady
PATSY KELLY
WALTER BRENNAN
FUZZY KNIGHT   MABEL TODD
HENRY KOLKER
Released by FILM CLASSICS Inc.

108

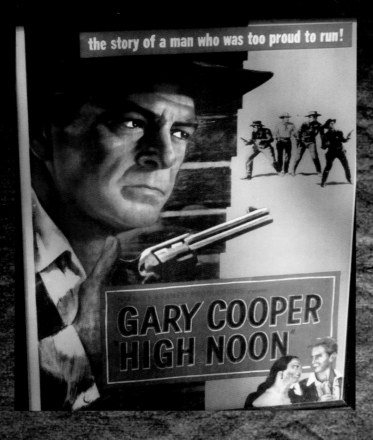

*"The Hanging Tree"*
**with Maria Schell**

Autographed photo - Estimated Value - $800.00 - $1000.00

"THE ROUNDERS"
A Metro-Goldwyn-Mayer Picture

65/29

Simon Fry observes the movement of some questionable characters, as Henry Fonda stars in TV's new adventure series, THE DEPUTY.

**mca**
TV FILM SYNDICATION

In "*Fire Creek*"
with Jimmy Stewart

# Murray 1908-1991

oto - Estimated Value - $400.00 - $600.00

with Barbera Stanwyck

113

**Clip Signature - Estimated Value**
**$300.00 - $400.00**

# Robert Preston   1918-1987

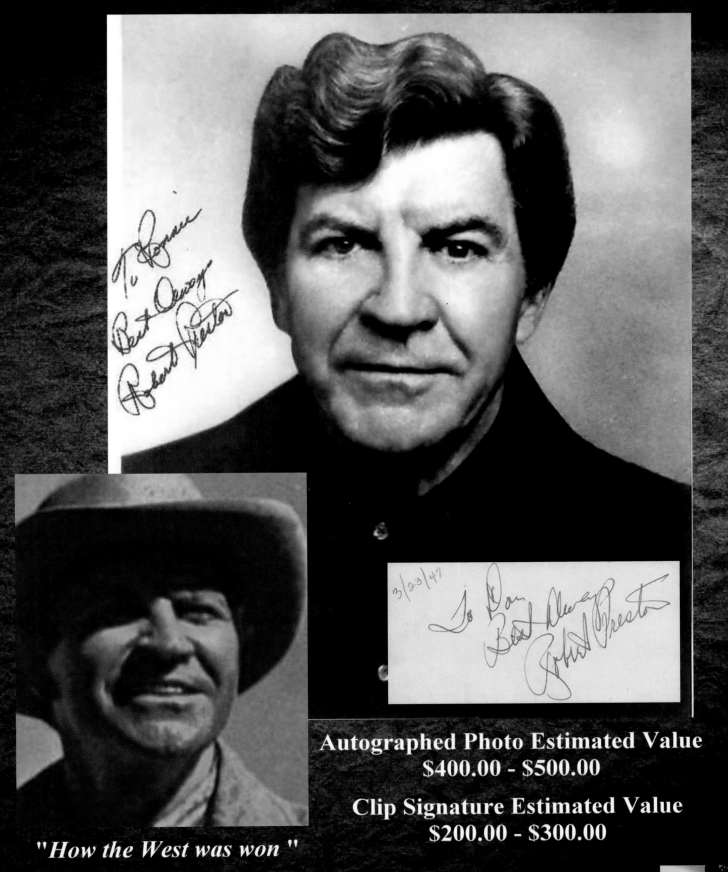

"How the West was won"

**Autographed Photo Estimated Value**
**$400.00 - $500.00**

**Clip Signature Estimated Value**
**$200.00 - $300.00**

# obert Young 1907-1998

**Clip Signature - Estimated Value - $200.00 - $300.00**

# Lloyd Nolan 1902-1985

with Jack Oakie

Clip Signature - Estimated Value -$300.00 - $400.00

# Ray Milland  1907-1986

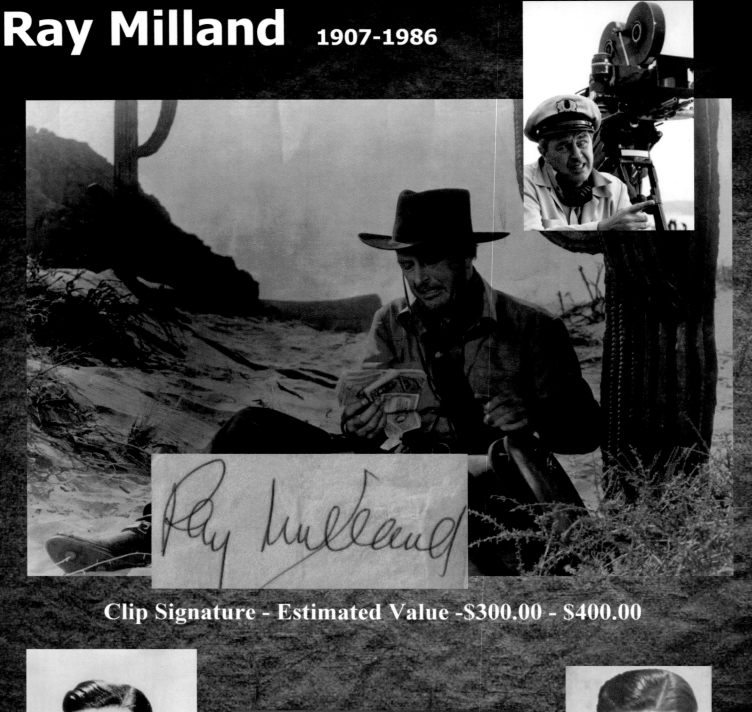

**Clip Signature - Estimated Value -$300.00 - $400.00**

**Autographed Photo - Estimated Value -$400.00 - $600.00**

118

# Robert Taylor 1911-1969

Autographed Photo
Estimated Value
$400.00 - $500.00

On set - "*Vaquero*"

tographed Photo - Estimated Value - $600.00 - $800.00

# John Payne
## 1912-1989

**Autographed Photo - Estimated Value - $300.00 - $500.00**

# Rory Calhoun 1922-1999

**Autographed Photo - Estimated Value - $300.00 - $500.00**

# Preston Foster 1900-1970

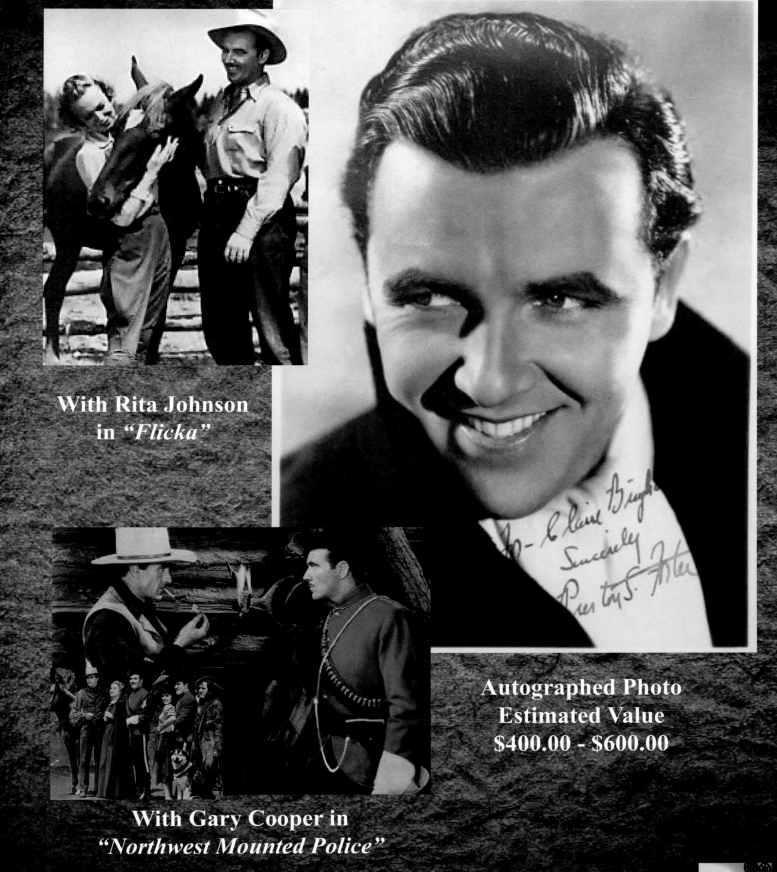

With Rita Johnson
in *"Flicka"*

With Gary Cooper in
*"Northwest Mounted Police"*

Autographed Photo
Estimated Value
$400.00 - $600.00

# Chapter Five
## 1950's & 60's - Later 'A' Westerns

# Gregory Peck 1916-2003

"McKenna's Gold"

**Clip Signature - Estimated Value - $400.00 - $600.00**

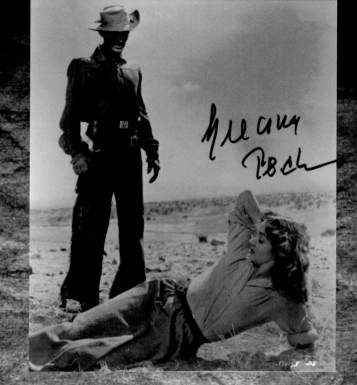

**Signed Photos - *"Duel in the Sun"*- $1,000.00 - $1,200.00 for both**

**2 Photos from**
***"The Bravados"***

# Robert Mitchum 1919-1997

**Autographed Photo - Estimated Value - $300.00 - $500.00**

## 2 Photos - *"Blood on the Moon"* with Barbara Belle Geddes

With Marilyn Monroe in

# Glenn Ford 1916-2006

**Autographed Photo - Estimated Value - $400.00 - $500.00**

Chief Dan George

Clip Signature - Estimated Value - $300.00 - $400.00

# Glenn Ford

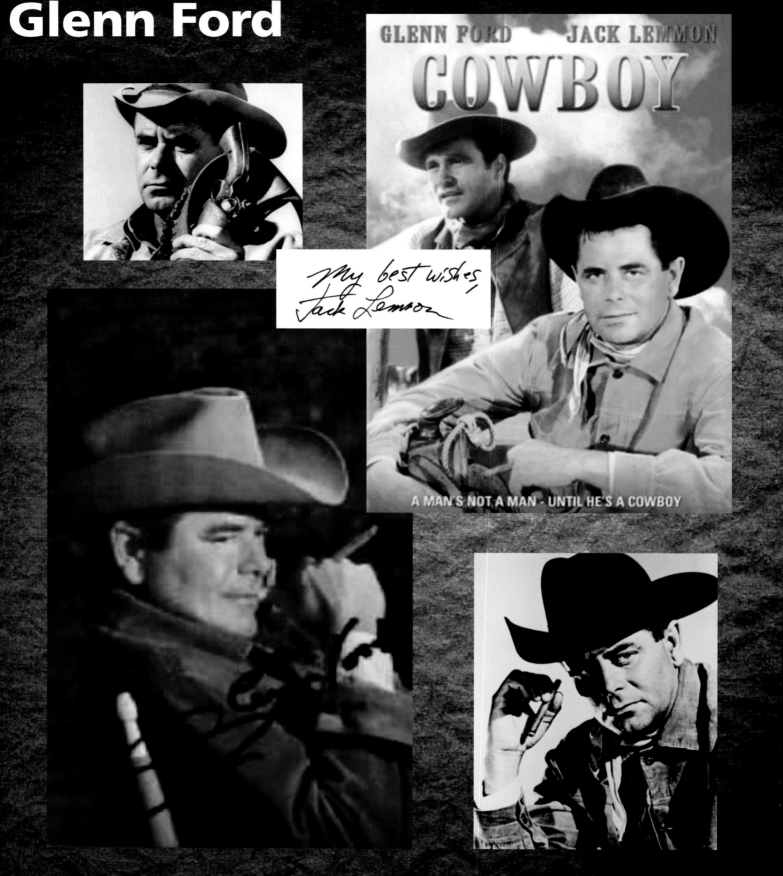

GLENN FORD    JACK LEMMON

COWBOY

A MAN'S NOT A MAN - UNTIL HE'S A COWBOY

My best wishes,
Jack Lemmon

**Autographed Photo - Estimated Value - $400.00 - $600.00**
**Clip Signature - Estimated Value - $200.00 - $400.00**

# William Holden 1918-1981

**Autographed Photo - Estimated Value - $400.00 - $600.00**

# Alan Ladd   1913-1964

**Autographed Photo - Estimated Value - $600.00 - $800.00**

*"Whispering Smith"*

**Set Photos from *"Shane"***

**Clip Signature - Estimated Value - $300.00 - $500.00**

# Burt Lancaster 1913-1994

From "*Hallelujah Trail*"

*Burt Lancaster*

**Clip Signature - Estimated Value - $400.00 - $500.00**

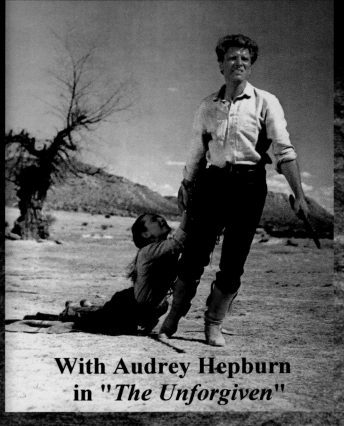

**With Audrey Hepburn in "*The Unforgiven*"**

**With Gary Cooper in "*Vera Cruz*"**

**Autographed Photo - Estimated Value - $800.00 - $1,000.00 - For both.**

# Charlton Heston 1923-2008

Copyright © 1967 by Paramount Pictures Corporation. All rights reserved. Permission granted for newspaper and magazine reproduction. (Made in U.S.A.)

**Technicolor®**

**"WILL PENNY"**
An Engel-Gries-Seltzer Production

PARAMOUNT PICTURE

Autographed Photo - Estimated Value - $400.00 - $600.00

Paramount Pictures Presents
CHARLTON HESTON · JOAN HACKETT · DONALD PLEASENCE
in
## "WILL PENNY"
Technicolor®                    A Paramount Picture
An Engle-Gries-Seltzer Production

68/5

# Jimmy Stewart 1908-1997

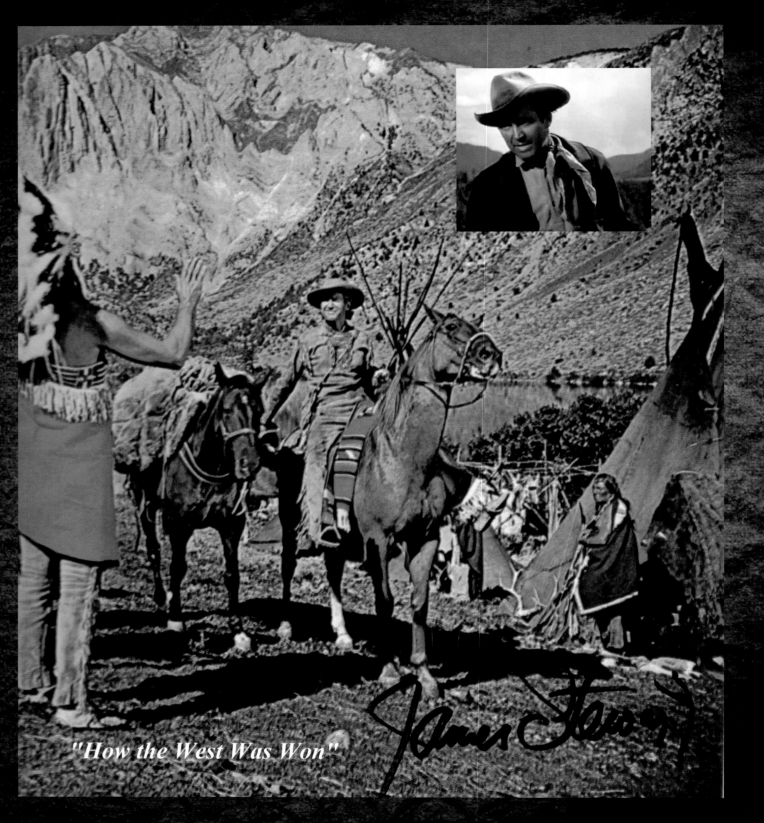

*"How the West Was Won"*

**Autographed Photo - Estimated Value - $400.00 - $600.00**

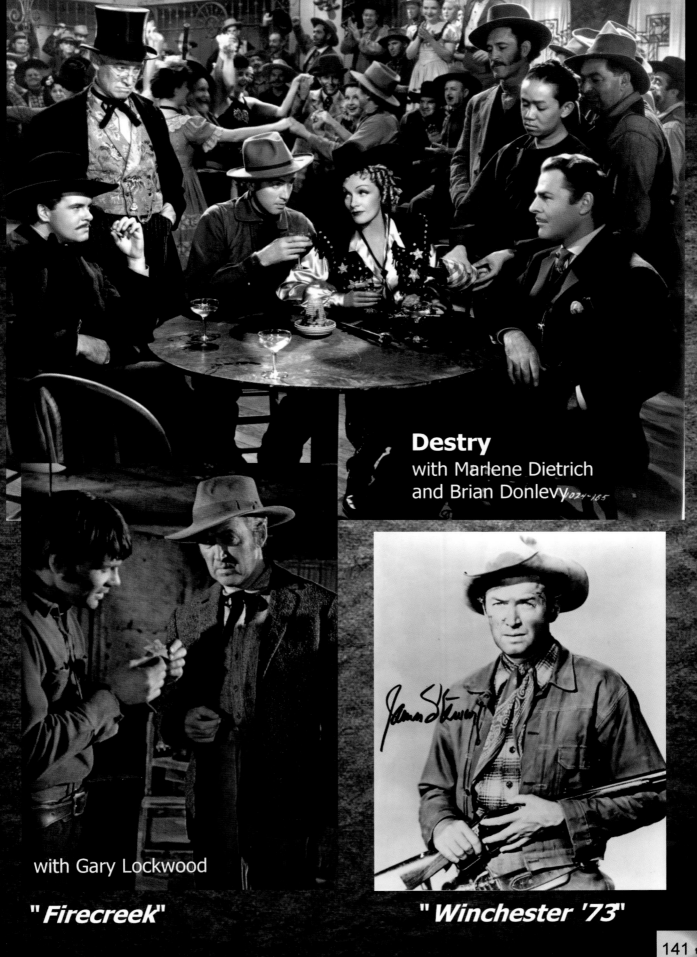

**Destry**
with Marlene Dietrich
and Brian Donlevy

with Gary Lockwood

" *Firecreek*"

" *Winchester '73*"

141

# Richard Widmark 1914-2008

**Autographed Photo - Estimated Value - $500.00 - $700.00**

COLUMBIA PICTURES Presents A SOL C. SIEGEL PRODUCTION WILLIAM HOLDEN · RICHARD WIDMARK
in ALVAREZ KELLY co-starring · JANICE RULE · VICTORIA SHAW · PATRICK O'NEAL · ROGER C. CARMEL
Produced by SOL C. SIEGEL · Directed by EDWARD DMYTRYK · PANAVISION® COLUMBIACOLOR

# oyd Bridges 1913-1998

**Autographed Photo - Estimated Value - $400.00 - $600.00**

*"High Noon"* with Katy Jurado, Gary Cooper, and Grace Kelly

With sons Jeff and Beau

2010 Remake of "True Grit"

# Kirk Douglas

**Autographed Photo - Estimated Value - $400.00 - $600.00**

**Matted Display $1,400.00 - $1,600.00**

**Autographed Photo - Estimated Value - $800.00 - $1,000.00**

# Erroll Flynn  1909-1959

with Olivia DeHaviland

Bruce Cabot and Victor Jory

**Clip Signature - Estimated Value - $800.00 - $1,000.00**

# Dick Powell 1909-1959

**Autographed Photo - Estimated Value - $700.00 - $900.00**

ROY
ROGERS
KING OF THE COWBOYS

# Chapter Six
## 1940's - 60's - Singing Cowboys

# Gene Autry 1907-1998

**Dick Jones**

REPUBLIC PICTURES presents **GENE AUTRY** in "GUNS AND GUITARS" with SMILEY BURNETTE and CHAMPION Produced by NAT LEVINE. PRINTED IN U.S.A.

**1940's (2) Autographed Photos - Estimated Value - $400.00 - $600.00 ea.**

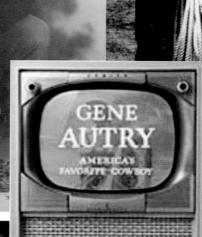

GENE
AUTRY
AMERICA'S
FAVORITE COWBOY

Gene AUTRY
AND COMPANY
IN PERSON
WITH HIS FAMOUS HORSE CHAMPION

Souvenir Program

# Roy Rogers & Dale Evans
## 1911-1998          1912-2001

**1980's (2) Autographs - Estimated Value - $600.00 - $800.00**

with Snuff Garrett

1980's (2) Autographs
Estimated Value
$400.00 - $500.00

Clip Signatures - $300.00 - $500.00

Roy Jr. Autograph
$100.00 - $200.00

# Rex Allen 1920-1999

**Autographed Photo - Estimated Value - $400.00 - $600.00**

**With Rex Jr, Roy Rogers,
and Snuff Garrett
(3) Signatues - $400.00 - $600.00**

**Photo with Signatures - Estimated Value - $2,000.00 - $2,500.00**

# Tex Ritter 1905-1974

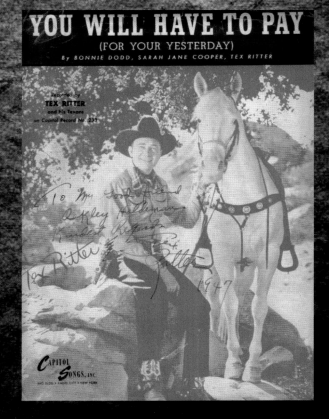

**Autographed Photo - Estimated Value - $500.00 - $600.00**

# Jimmy Wakely    1914-1982

With
Dub Taylor

Autographed Photo - Estimated Value - $200.00 - $400.00

# Ray Whitley    1901-1979

# Eddie Dean
## 1907-1999

**Autographed Photo - Estimated Value - $300.00 - $400.00**

To Ken
my Friend
The End

Monte Hale
Much Love Pal

**Autographed Photo - Estimated Value - $300.00 - $400.00**

**Autographed Photo - Estimated Value - $300.00 - $400.00**

# Tex Williams 1917-1985

**Autographed Photo - Estimated Value - $400.00 - $500.00**

## Sheet Music - Estimated Value - $50.00 - $100.00

## (5) Autographed Photos - Estimated Value - $200.00 - $400.00

# Bob Baker 1914-1975

**Autographed Photo - Estimated Value - $300.00 - $400.00**

**(6) 1941 Clip Signatures - matching photo**
**Estimated Value - $1,000.00 - $1,200.00 (for all)**

**Bob Nolan**

**Founders, "Sons of the Pioneers" left to right**
**Tim Spencer, Bob Nolan, Karl Farr, & Roy Rogers**
**Photo - Estimated Value - $100.00 - $200.00**

**(1)**

**(3)**

Sons of the Pioneers

**This group Photo**
**$300.00 - $500.00**

**(2)**

**(4)**

**(4) Different groups of "The Sons of the Pioneers"**

# pade Cooley 1910-1969

Sincerely,

Spade

**Clip Signature
-Estimated Value
-$300.00 - $400.00**

**Spade Cooley Orchestra,
(Tex Williams far right.)**

**Spade Cooley Citation**
**Signed by (9) Sons of the Pioneers**
**$500.00 - $600.00**

**Signed Contract**
**$300.00 - $400.00**

**Bob Wills signed letter to Spade Cooley-$600.00 - $800.00**

# Merle Travis    1917-1983

Autographed Photo - Estimated Value -$300.00 - $400.00

# Doye O'Dell & Pee Wee King
## 1912-2001            1914-2000

(2) Autographed Photo - Estimated Value -$100.00 - $200.00 ea.

# Chapter Seven
## 1940's - 60's - Western Sidekicks

# Gabby Hayes 1889-1969

Autographed Photo - Estimated Value - 300.00 - $400.00

Clip Signature
Estimated Value
$300.00 - $400.00

# Smiley Burnette 1911-1967

**Autographed Photo - Estimated Value - 300.00 - $400.00**

With the Author in the 1950's

**Autographed Sheet Music - Estimated Value - 300.00 - $400.00**

# Pat Buttram 1915-1994

**Autographed Photo - Estimated Value - $300.00 - $400.00**
**Clip Signature - $100.00 - $200.00**

# dy Devine 1905-1977

**Autographed Photo - Estimated Value - $200.00 - $300.00**

# Slim Pickens 1919-1983

Slim

Dear Vernon,
Sure good to hear from
you. Thanks a lot. I messed
up one of your pictures so
I replaced it. Hope thats
O.K.

Sincerely,
Slim Pickens

**Autographed Photo - Estimated Value - $300.00 - $400.00**
**Signed Letter - Estimated Value - $200.00 - $300.00**

# Pat Brady 1914-1972

**Clip Signature**
**$100.00 - $200.00**

**Sunset Serenade 1942**
**Back: Tim Spencer, Karl Farr and Pat Brady**
**Front: Bob Nolan, Lloyd Perryman and Hugh Farr**

# Dub Taylor 1907-1994

As Cannonball Taylor

Character Actor

Buck Taylor on the set of *"Gunsmoke"*

Dub's son Buck Taylor is also an Artist.

Autographed Photo - Estimated Value - $200.00- $300.00

# Max Terhune
## 1891-1973

*To Jimmy Widener a good comedian and I enjoyed trouping with you.*

*enjoyed it also. You really know how to "time" your gags. your pal "Elmer" "your Pal" Max Terhune "lullaby"*

With "Banjo"

**Autographed Photo - Estimated Value - $100.00- $200.00**

# Raymond Hatton 1887-1971

Autographed Photo - Estimated Value - $200.00- $300.00

Buck Jones with Tim McCoy and Raymond Hatton
as the 'Rough Riders'. Together they made 8 films for Monogram.

# Andy Clyde
### 1892-1967

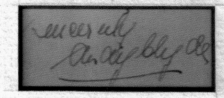

**Autographed Photo - Estimated Value - $200.00 - $300.00**
**Clip Signature - Estimated Value - $100.00 - $200.00**

# Al "Fuzzy" St. John 1893-1963

With Lash LaRue

**Autograph Not Shown - Estimated Value Signed - $100.00 - $200.00**

# Eddie Waller  1889-1977

Shown with Ruth Roman and Jimmy Stewart

Autograph Not Shown - Estimated Value Signed - $200.00 - $300.00

FUZZY KNIGHT

# Emmett Lynn 1897-1958

**Autograph Not Shown - Estimated Value Signed - $100.00 - $200.00**

from "Colorado Serenade" with Eddie Dean,
Mary Kenyon and Charlies King.

"PRAIRIE OUTLAWS" with EDDIE DEAN and his horse FLASH.
ROSCOE ATES, SARAH PADDEN and AL LaRUE
A PRC Production

48/999

5-92-35

Autographed Photo Estimated Value $100.00 $200.00

# Chapter Eight
## 1940's - 60's - Western Heavies

# Roy Barcroft 1902-1969

No Autograph Shown - Estimated Value Signed - $300.00 - $400.00

# Harry Woods 1889-1968

**With Roy Barcroft**

**No Autograph Shown - Estimated Value Signed - $300.00 - $400.00**

...th Deul Bryant, Ed Cobb, George Cheseboro and Charles Starrett

©CP CORP D-COL.309-23

No Autograph Shown - Estimated Value Signed - $200.00 - $300.00

Autograph Not Shown – Estimated Value Signed – $200.00 – $300.00

# George Chesebro 1888-1959

Standing 2nd From Right.

**Autograph Not Shown - Estimated Value Signed - $200.00 - $300.00**

# Robert J. Wilke    1914-1989

**Autographed Photo - Estimated Value - $200.00 - $300.00**

# ohn Merton 1901-1959

© Republic Pictures Corporation. Leased only to exhibitors having license to exhibit above entitled motion pictures, and only for display in connection therewith; must not be otherwise used, sold, leased or disposed of. Reproduction permitted only by newspapers and magazines and only if credited by them to said motion picture.

"ZORRO'S BLACK WHIP," with GEORGE J. LEWIS, LINDA STIRLING. A REPUBLIC RE-RELEASE IN 12 CHAPTERS. PRINTED IN U.S.A. R57/5805

**Autograph Not Shown - Estimated Value Signed - $100.00 - $200.00**

# Leo Gordon

**1922-2000**

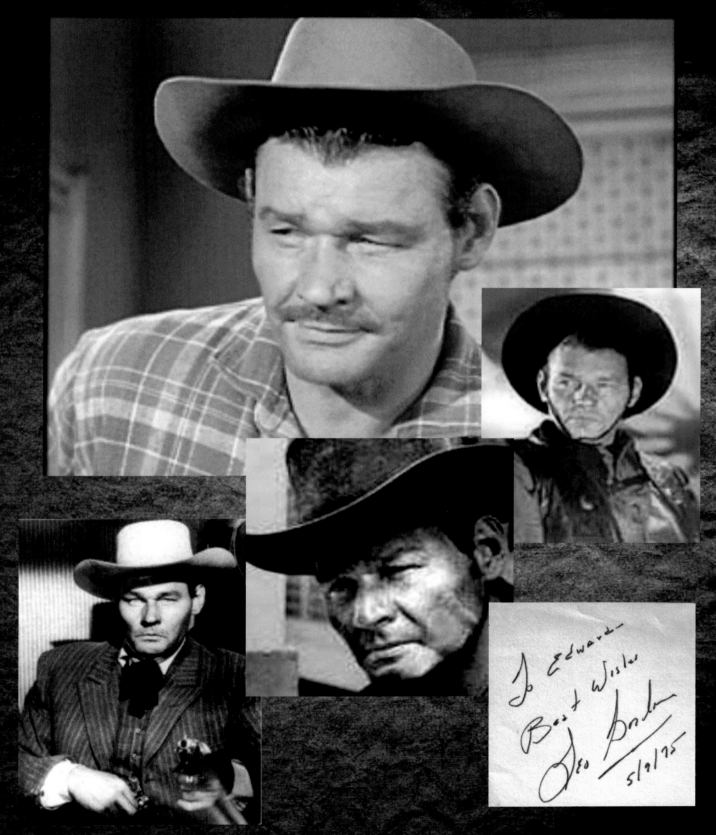

**Clip Signature - Estimated Value - $200.00 - $300.00**
**Autograph Not Shown - Estimated Value Signed - $300.00 - $500.00**

# Terry Frost 1906-1993

**Autographed Photo - Estimated Value   - $300.00 - $400.00**

# LeRoy Mason  1903-1947

**Bottom right with Bud Geary, Hal Taliaferro, and Kenne Duncan**
**Autograph Not Shown - Estimated Value Signed   - $100.00 - $200.00**

# Walter Miller 1892-1940

Autograph Not Shown - Estimated Value Signed  - $100.00 - $200.00

# Tris Coffin
## 1909-1990

**Autographed Photo - Estimated Value - $200.00 - $300.00**

# John Doucette 1921-1994

Autographed Photo - Estimated Value - $200.00 - $300.00

# enneth MacDonald 1901-1972

Autograph Not Shown - Estimated Value Signed - $200.00 - $300.00

# Brian Donlevy 1901-1972

**Autographed Photo - Estimated Value - $200.00 - $300.00**

# Chapter Nine
## 1940's - 60's - Good/Bad Guys

With Best Wishes —

*Lee Marvin*

Cast of "Cat Ballou"

221

# Richard Boone 1917-1981

**Autographed Photo - Estimated Value  - $400.00 - $600.00**

**Clip Signature - Estimated Value  - $300.00 - $500.00**

223

# Jack Elam 1920-2003

Autographed Photo - Estimated Value  - $400.00 - $600.00

224

# Gilbert Roland

**1905-1994**

THE FURIES

23e

**Autographed Photo - Estimated Value - $200.00 - $400.00**

# Cesar Romero 1904-1994

With Jean Rogers

_Yours truly_
_Cesar Romero_

73

**Autographed Photo - Estimated Value - $200.00 - $400.00**

For the Dear Family
Best Wishes
Eli Wallach

Tuco

Autographed Photo - Estimated Value  - $400.00 - $600.00

for Thomas Hermann
Best wishes
Eli Wallach

TUCO

# Nehemiah Persoff

Autographed Photo - Estimated Value  - $300.00 - $400.00
Clip Signature - Estimated Value - $300.00 - $400.00

# Lee Van Cleef   1925-1989

**Autographed Photo - Estimated Value  - $300.00 - $500.00**

# Claude Akins
## 1926-1994

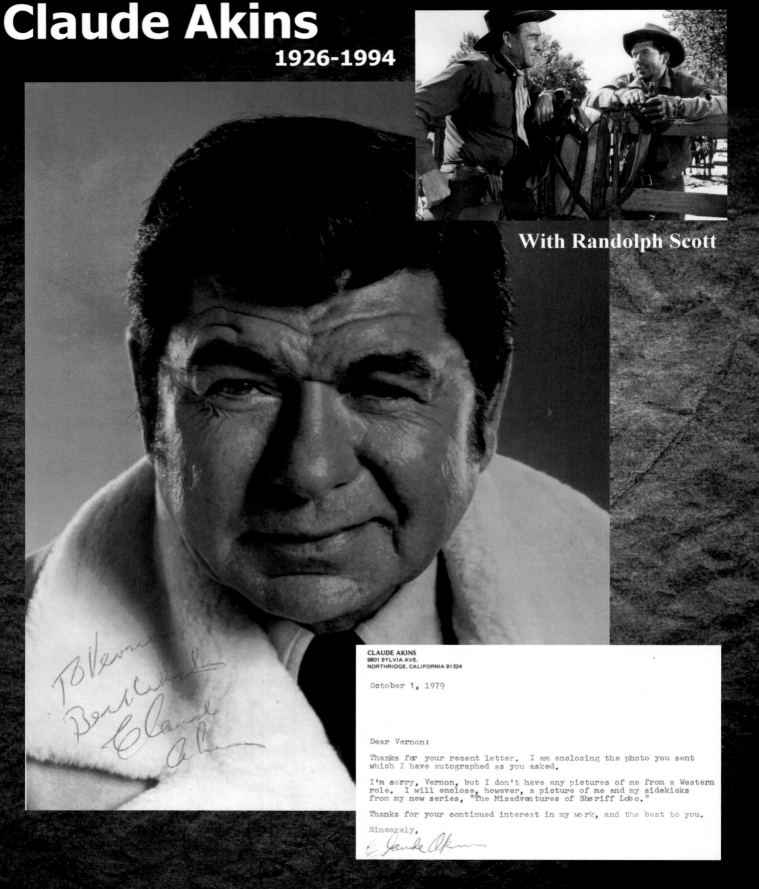

**With Randolph Scott**

CLAUDE AKINS
9801 SYLVIA AVE.
NORTHRIDGE, CALIFORNIA 91324

October 1, 1979

Dear Vernon:

Thanks for your recent letter. I am enclosing the photo you sent which I have autographed as you asked.

I'm sorry, Vernon, but I don't have any pictures of me from a Western role. I will enclose, however, a picture of me and my sidekicks from my new series, "The Misadventures of Sheriff Lobo."

Thanks for your continued interest in my work, and the best to you.

Sincerely,

**Autographed Photo - Estimated Value - $400.00 - $600.00**
**Signed Letter - $300.00 - $500.00**

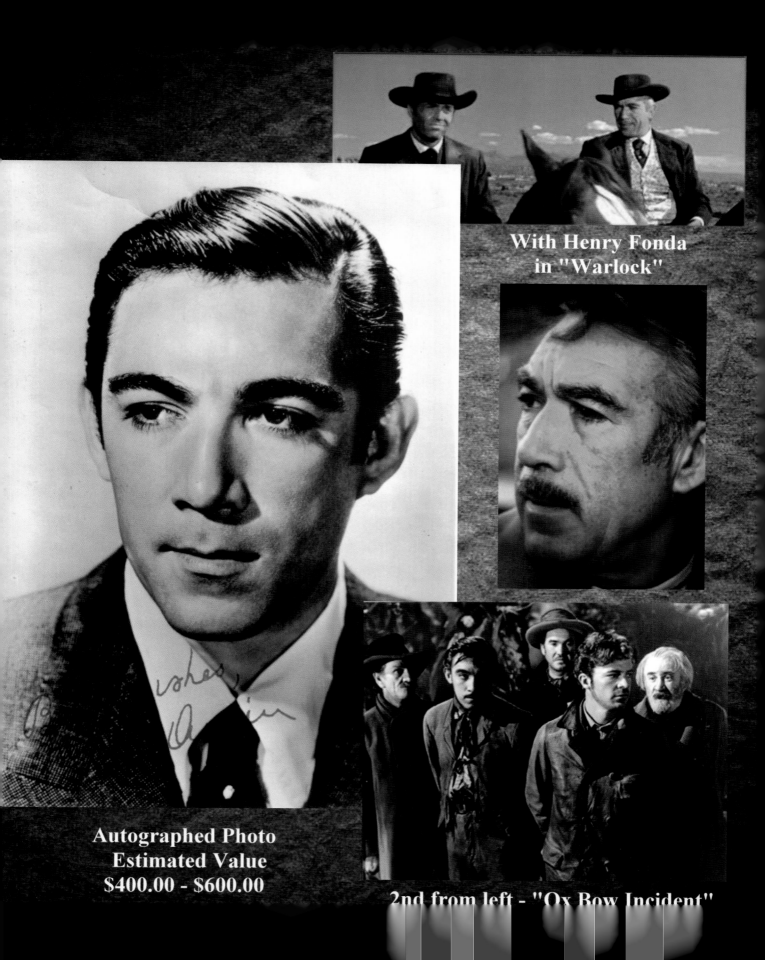

With Henry Fonda
in "Warlock"

Autographed Photo
Estimated Value
$400.00 - $600.00

2nd from left - "Ox Bow Incident"

# Victor Jory 1902-1982

**Clip Signature - Estimated Value - $300.00 - $500.00**

# John Ireland
## 1914-1992

"I Shot Jesse James"

"Red River"

with Montgomery Clift

With Wife Joanne Dru above.
**Double Autographed Photo - Estimated Value - $300.00 - $500.00**

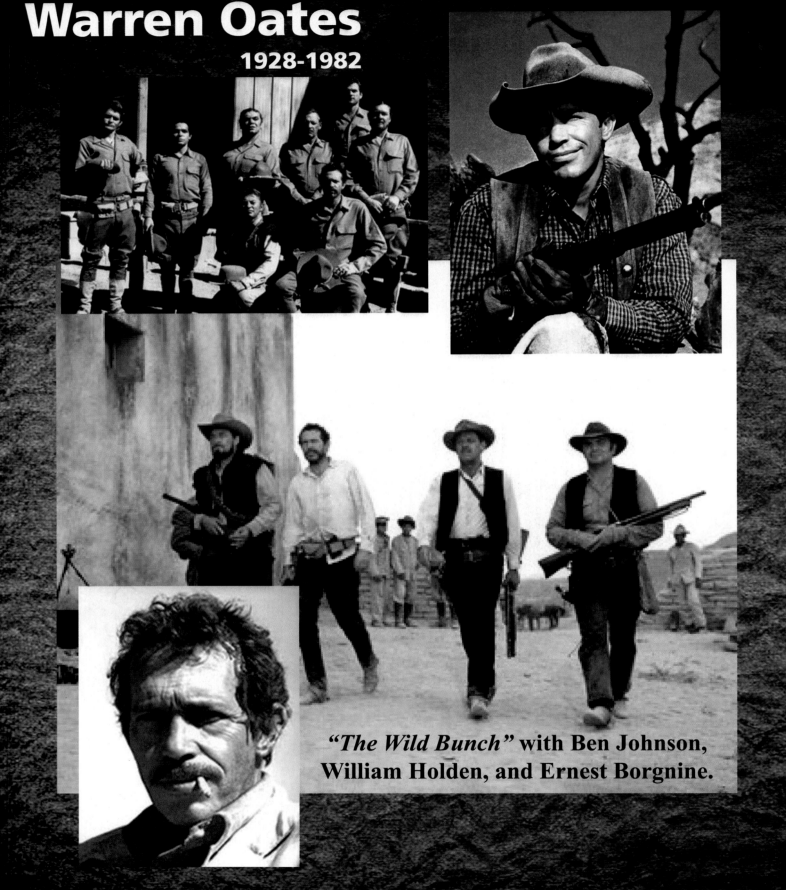

# Warren Oates
## 1928-1982

*"The Wild Bunch"* with Ben Johnson, William Holden, and Ernest Borgnine.

Autographed Not Shown - Estimated Value Signed - $200.00 - $300.00

# Victor French 1934-1989

**Autographed Photo - Estimated Value - $200.00 - $300.00**
**Clip Signature - Estimated Value - $100.00 - $200.00**

237

# Richard Jaeckel 1926-1997

Best always,
Richard Jaeckel

**Autograph Not Shown - Estimated Value Signed - $300.00 - $400.00**
**Clip Signature - Estimated Value - $200.00 - $300.00**

# obert Lowery 1913-1971

*Robert Lowery*

*Bob Lowery*

**Autograph Photo - Estimated Value  - $100.00 - $200.00**
**Clip Signatures - Estimated Value - $100.00 - $200.00**

# Chapter Ten
## 1930's - 60's - Indians in Westerns

# Iron Eyes Cody  1904-1999

**Autographed Photo - Estimated Value  - $200.00 - $300.00**

# Jay Silverheels 1912-1980

Clip Signature - Estimated Value - $400.00 - $600.00

243

# Monte Blue  1887-1963

**Autographed Photo - Estimated Value - $300.00 - $400.00**

244

# Chief Yowlachie 1891-1966

**Autograph Not Shown - Estimated Value Signed - $300.00 - $400.00**

# Charlie Stevens 1893-1964

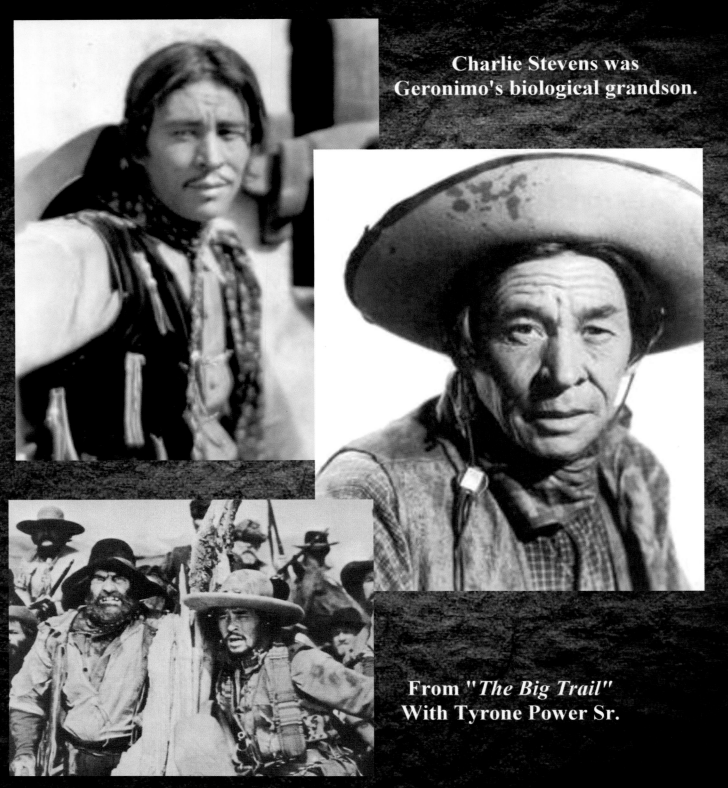

Charlie Stevens was
Geronimo's biological grandson.

From "*The Big Trail*"
With Tyrone Power Sr.

Autograph Not Shown - Estimated Value Signed  - $200.00 - $300.00

# Chief Thundercloud

**1899-1955**

With Lee Powell
in the Lone Ranger Serial.

Autograph Not Shown - Estimated Value Signed - $200.00 - $300.00

247

Rodd Redwing was a Chickasaw Indian. He taught the star how to shoot for over 30 years, supervised gunfight scenes, and taught the actors how to handle their guns.

Autographed Photo - Estimated Value - $200.00 - $300.00

# Jim Thorpe
## 1888-1953

**"OUTLAW TRAIL" 1944**

2nd from left with Hoot Gibson, Al Fergusson, Frank Ellis and Chief Thundercloud.

With Carl Laemmle

*The Red Rider* Heavies: Jim Corey, Richard Cramer, Walter Miller, Monte Montague, Art Ortega, Bud Osborne, *Jim Thorpe* and Al Fergusson.

**Autograph Not Shown - Estimated Value Signed - $300.00 - $400.00**

# Nipo Strongheart 1891-1966

2nd from the right with Tyrone Power, Frank Dekova,
Adeline De Walt Reynolds and John Wareagle
"Pony Soldiers" 1952

**Michael Horse**

**X. Brands**

**Barbara Hershey**

**Autograph Not Shown - Estimated Value Signed - $100.00 - $200.00**

250

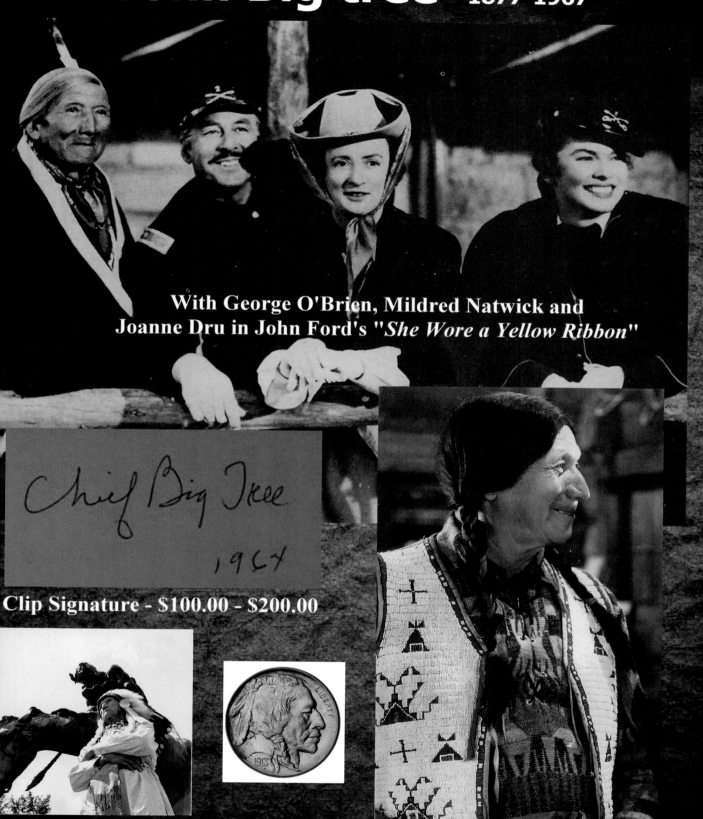

# Chief John Big tree
## 1877-1967

With George O'Brien, Mildred Natwick and
Joanne Dru in John Ford's "*She Wore a Yellow Ribbon*"

*Chief Big Tree*
*1954*

**Clip Signature - $100.00 - $200.00**

Chief Big Tree claimed to have posed for both the Indian
head nickel and Fraser's "End of the Trail" statue.

# Will Sampson

**1933-1987**

Autograph Not Shown - Estimated Value Signed - $200.00 - $300.00

# Chief Dan George 1899-1981

**Autographed Photo - Estimated Value - $300.00 - $400.00**

# Wes Studi

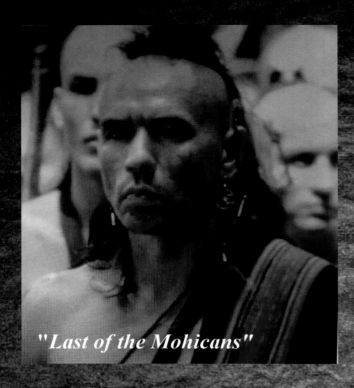

"Last of the Mohicans"

"Dances With Wolves"

"Geronimo"

Autographed Photo - Estimated Value - $300.00 - $400.00

# Eddie Little Sky 1926-1997

Eddie Little Sky as 'Chief of Crow' in the 1965 movie, "The Hallelujah Trail".

With the author in Cody, Wyoming in 1990

To - Ken
May the Great Spirit make Sunshine in your Heart always
Your Friend
Eddie Little Sky
Cody Wyo - 90

Eddie Little Sky
Dawn Little Sky

Clip Signature - Estimated Value - $100.00 - $200.00 ea.

# Floyd Westerman
## 1936-2007

*"Dances with Wolves"*
co-star Rodney A. Grant

Autograph Not Shown - Estimated Value Signed - $200.00 - $300.00
Autographed Photo - Rodney A. Grant - $200.00 - $300.00

# Graham Green

Autograph Not Shown - Estimated Value Signed - $200.00 - $300.00

# Chapter Eleven
## 1930's - 60's - Women in Westerns

# Virginia Mayo   1920-2005

Virginia Mayo

**Autographed Photo - Estimated Value - $200.00 - $300.00**

# Barbara Stanwyck 1907-1990

"Union Pacific"

**Clip Signature - Estimated Value - $200.00 - $300.00**

**Autographed Photo - Estimated Value - $300.00 - $400.00**

# Ella Raines   1920-1988

**Autographed Photo - Estimated Value - $200.00 - $300.00**

# Ann Baxter 1923-1985

**Autographed Photo - Estimated Value - $200.00 - $300.00**

# Marie Windsor

**1919-2000**

**Autographed Photo - Estimated Value - $300.00 - $400.00**

# Yvonne DeCarlo  1922-2007

Good Luck! Yvonne DeCarlo

**Autographed Photo - Estimated Value - $300.00 - $400.00**

266

# Rhonda Fleming

To Henry + Genevieve,
It was a pleasure
meeting you both!
Warmest regards –
Rhonda Fleming
'90

**Autographed Photo - Estimated Value - $300.00 - $400.00**

# Cecilia Parker 1914-1993

**Autographed Photo - Estimated Value - $100.00 - $200.00**

268

# Claire Trevor
### 1910-2000

**Autographed Photo - Estimated Value - $100.00 - $200.00**

# Jane Russell

Autographed Photo - Estimated Value - $200.00 - $300.00

# Marlene Dietrich 1901-1992

**Autographed Photo - Estimated Value - $200.00 - $300.00**

# Joanne Dru 1922-1996

**Autographed Photo - Estimated Value - $200.00 - $300.00**

# Maureen O'hara

**Autographed Photo - Estimated Value - $200.00 - $300.00**

# Barbara Britton 1919-1980

**Autographed Photo - Estimated Value - $200.00 - $300.00**

# Vera Miles

**Autographed Photo - Estimated Value - $200.00 - $300.00**

# Jean Arthur
## 1900-1991

**With Gary Cooper in "*The Plainsman*"**

**With Alan Ladd in "*Shane*"**

**Autographed Photo - Estimated Value - $200.00 - $300.00**

# Peggy Stewart

With
Gene Autry

**Autographed Photo - Estimated Value - $200.00 - $300.00**

# Chapter Twelve
## Post-1960's "A" Westerns

Autographed Photo - Estimated Value - $400.00 - $500.00

# Clint Eastwood

## 50 years of Western Movies

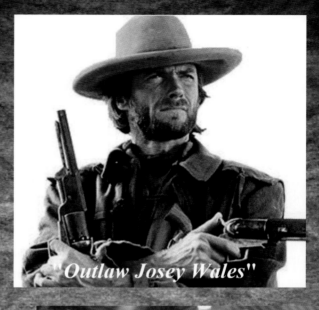

*"Outlaw Josey Wales"*

*"A Fistfull of Dollars"*

*"Bronco Billy"*

*"Hang 'em High"*

*"Joe Kidd"*

*"Unforgiven"*

281

# Kevin Costner

**Autographed Photo - Estimated Value - $300.00 - $400.00**

# Steve McQueen 1930-1980

**Autographed Photo - Estimated Value - $600.00 - $800.00**

# Sam Elliott

To Rodney, All the best, Sam Elliott

All the best! Katherine Ross

All THE BEST ALWAYS— Sam Elliott

**Autographed Photo - Estimated Value - $200.00 - $400.00**
**Clip Signatures - Estimated Value - $200.00 - $300.00 For both.**

# Charles Bronson 1921-2003

**Autographed Photo - Estimated Value - $400.00 - $600.00**

# Tom Selleck

**Autographed Photo - Estimated Value - $300.00 - $500.00**

Best Wishes
Tom Selleck

# Paul Newman 1925-2008

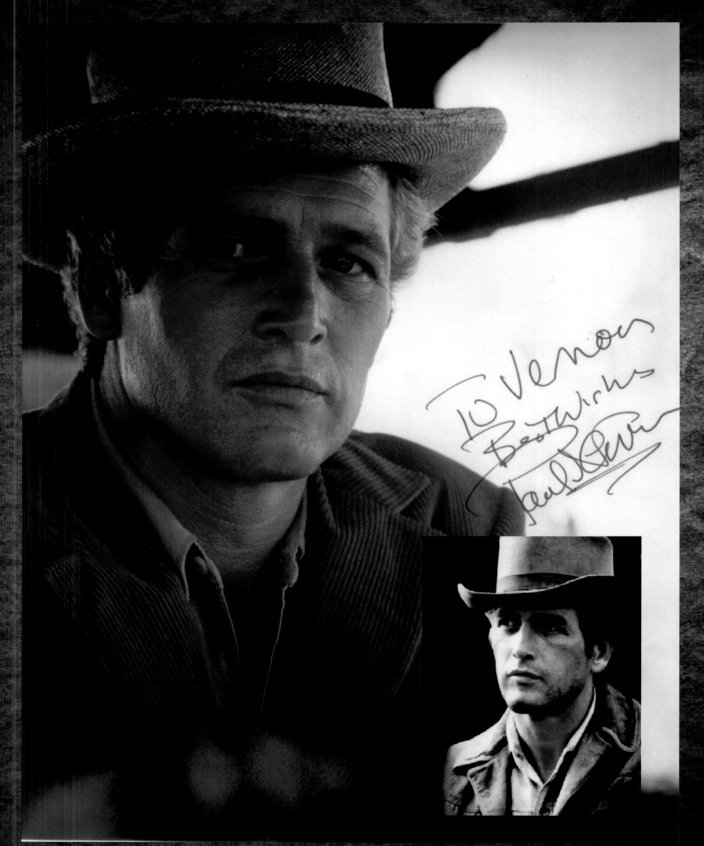

**Autographed Photo - Estimated Value - $600.00 - $800.00**

# Robert Redford

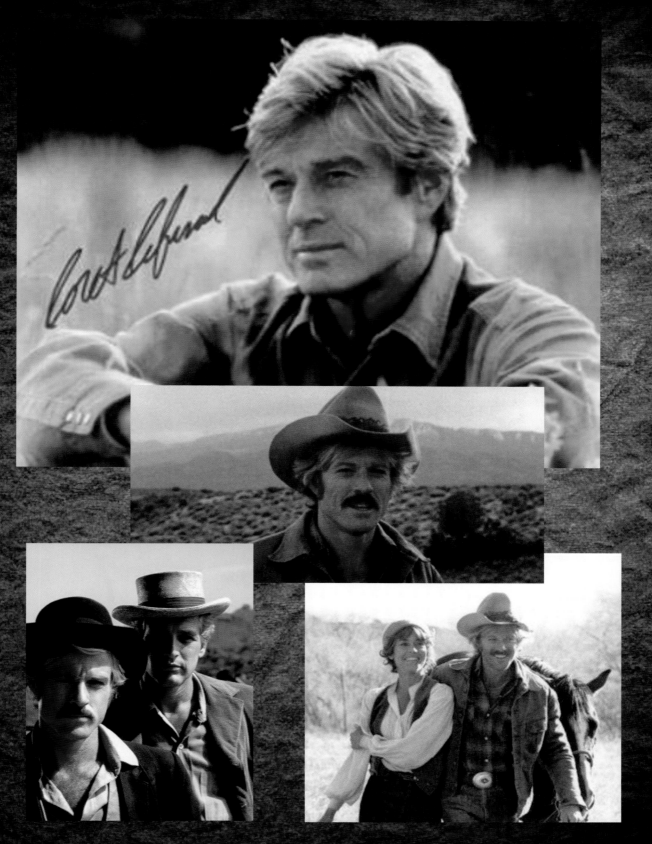

Autographed Photo - Estimated Value - $400.00 - $600.00

# Kurt Russell

*"The Quest"*

Kurt's father Bing Russell was a "B"
western supporting actor in many films.

Bing Russell

Autographed Photo - Estimated Value - $400.00 - $600.00

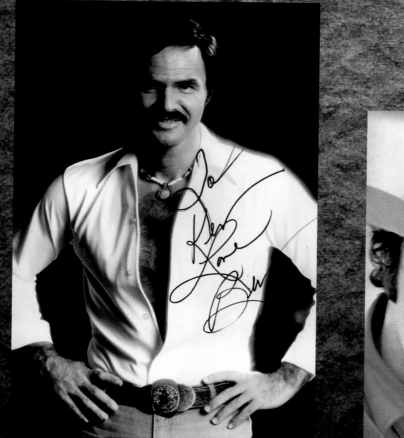

Autographed Photo - Estimated Value - $200.00 - $300.00

# James Coburn 1928-2002

Autographed Photo - Estimated Value - $300.00 - $400.00

# Tom Berenger

*"Last of the Dogmen"*

*"Rustler's Rhapsody"*

*"Last of the Dogmen"* with Barbara Hershey

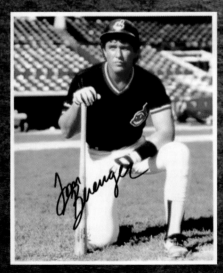

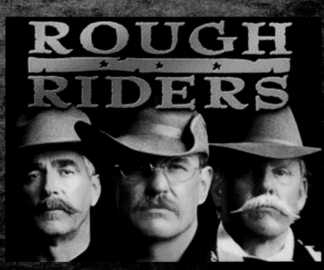

**Autographed Photo - Estimated Value - $200.00 - $300.00**
**Clip Signature - Estimated Value - $100.00 - $200.00**

# Rock Hudson
## 1925-1985

Autographed Photo - Estimated Value - $200.00 - $300.00

# Yul Brynner 1920-1985

**As Poncho Villa**

*"Catlow"*

# Val Kilmer

**Autographed Photo - Estimated Value - $300.00 - $500.00**
**Clip Signature - Estimated Value - $100.00 - $300.00**

# Robert Duvall

**Autographed Photo - Estimated Value - $300.00 - $500.00**

297

# Chapter Thirteen
## 1940's-70's Veteran Western Actors

# Walter Brennan 1894-1974

**Clip Signature - Estimated Value - $200.00 - $300.00**

THE GUNS OF WILL SONNETT

"THE PARIAH"

A
THOMAS/SPELLING PRODUCTION
780 North Gower Street
Hollywood, California 90038

**Signed Script
Estimated Value
$300.00 - $500.00**

**$100.00 - $200.00**

# Chill Wills 1902-1978

**Autographed Photo - Estimated Value - $200.00 - $300.00**

# William Fawcett 1894-1974

"FURY"

With Peter Graves and Bobby Diamond

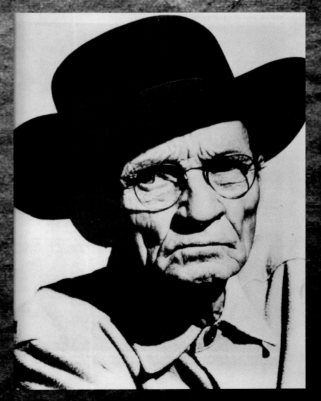

Autograph Not Shown - Estimated Value Signed - $100.00 - $200.00

# Charles Bickford 1891-1967

With Jennifer Jones in *"Duel in the Sun"*

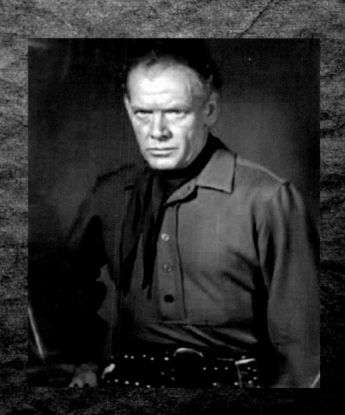

Autograph Not Shown - Estimated Value Signed - $100.00 - $200.00

# Lionel Barrymore
## 1878-1954

**(2) Photos from "Duel in the Sun"**

**Autographed Photo - Estimated Value - $300.00 - $500.00**

# John McIntire 1907-1991

**Autographed Photo - Estimated Value - $200.00 - $300.00**

# ay Teal    1902-1976

**Autographed Photo - Estimated Value - $300.00 - $400.00**

# Will Geer 1902-1978

**Autographed Photo - Estimated Value - $200.00 - $300.00**

# Raymond Massey

**1896-1983**

**Autographed Photo - Estimated Value - $300.00 - $500.00**

# Thomas Mitchell
## 1892-1962

Autograph Not Shown - Estimated Value Signed - $200.00 - $300.00
Clip Signature - Estimated Value - $100.00 - $200.00

# Paul Fix
## 1901-1983

With John Wayne 1933

**Autographed Photo - Estimated Value - $200.00 - $300.00**

# John Carradine
## 1906-1988

*"Stagecoach"*

Sons Robert,
David & Keith.

Autograph Not Shown - Estimated Value Signed - $200.00 - $300.00
Clip Signature - Estimated Value - $100.00 - $200.00

# Victor Mc Laglen  1886-1959

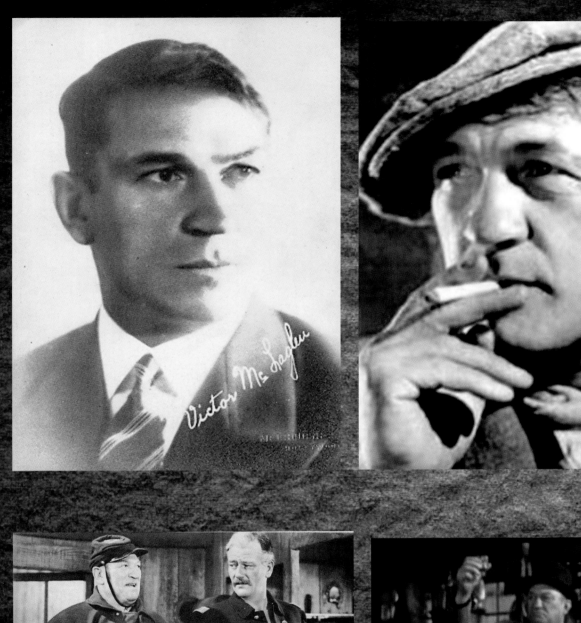

**Autographed Photo - Estimated Value  - $200.00 - $300.00**

# Walter Huston  1884-1950

**Autograph Not Shown - Estimated Value Signed - $300.00 - $400.00**
**Clip Signature - Estimated Value - $200.00 - $300.00**

# Edgar Buchanan
## 1903-1979

With Howard Duff in
*"Red Canyon"*

**Autographed Photo (Buchanan) - Estimated Value - $200.00 - $300.00**
**Autographed Photo (Duff) - Estimated Value - $300.00 - $400.00**

# Chapter Fourteen

## 1940's-70's Supporting Western Actors

# Forrest Tucker

**1919-1986**

**Autographed Photo - Estimated Value  - $300.00 - $500.00**
**Double Autograph - Estimated Value - $400.00 - $600.00**

# Arthur Kennedy
## 1914-1990

Photo Below with Jimmy Stewart and Rock Hudson from *"Bend of the River"*

(4) Photos above from *"Rancho Notorious"* with Mel Ferrer and Marlene Dietrich.

Autographed Photo - Estimated Value - $200.00 - $300.00
Clip Signature - Estimated Value - $200.00 - $300.00

Autographed Photo - Estimated Value - $300.00 - $400.00

# MacDonald Carey 1913-1994

**Autographed Photo - Estimated Value - $300.00 - $400.00**

321

Starring
SCOTT BRADY

Autographed Photo  Estimated Value   $300.00 - $400.00

# Steve Cochran  1917-1965

**With Gary Cooper
and Ruth Roman**

**Autographed Photo - Estimated Value  - $300.00 - $400.00**

# Denver Pyle  1920-1997

**Autographed Photo - Estimated Value  - $300.00 - $400.00**

# James Best

"Fire Creek"

"Ride Lonesome"

Autographed Photo - Estimated Value - $300.00 - $400.00

# Ben Johnson

**1918-1996**

*To my good friend Vernon*
*Ben Johnson*

**Autographed Photo - Estimated Value - $300.00 - $500.00**

# John Agar 1921-2002

**Autographed Photo - Estimated Value - $200.00 - $300.00**

# Harry Carey Jr.

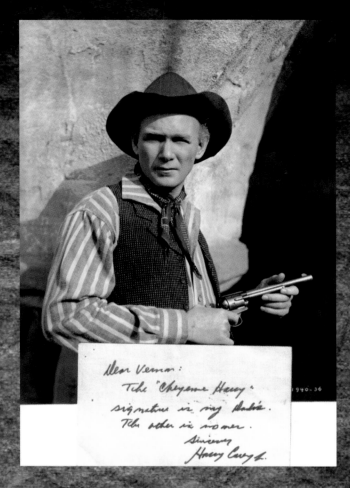

**Autographed Photo - Estimated Value  - $100.00 - $200.00**

# Noah Beery Jr. 1913-1994

Noah Jr.

Wallace Beery

Noah Sr.

Autographed Photos - Estimated Value - $300.00 - $400.00 each

# Jim Davis 1909-1981

**Autograph Not Shown - Estimated Value Signed - $300.00 - $400.00**

With John Wayne in *"The Searchers"*

Clip Signature - Estimated Value - $300.00 - $400.00

# Edmund O'Brien 1915-1985

With Jimmy Stewart and John Wayne in *"The Man Who Shot Liberty Valance"*

Autographed Photo - Estimated Value - $300.00 - $400.00

# James Whitmore 1921-2009

Best wishes,
James Whitmore

For Peter
You can't beat good bloodlines
Warmly
James Whitmore

**Autographed Photo - Estimated Value - $300.00 - $400.00**
**Clip Signature - Estimated Value - $200.00 - $300.00**

333

# Chapter Fifteen
## 1950's-70's Western T.V. Actors

# James Arness - "*Gunsmoke*"

Howdy
Vernon
your friend
Jim Arness

**Autographed Photo - Estimated Value - $300.00 - $500.00**
**Clip Signature - Estimated Value - $200.00 - $300.00**

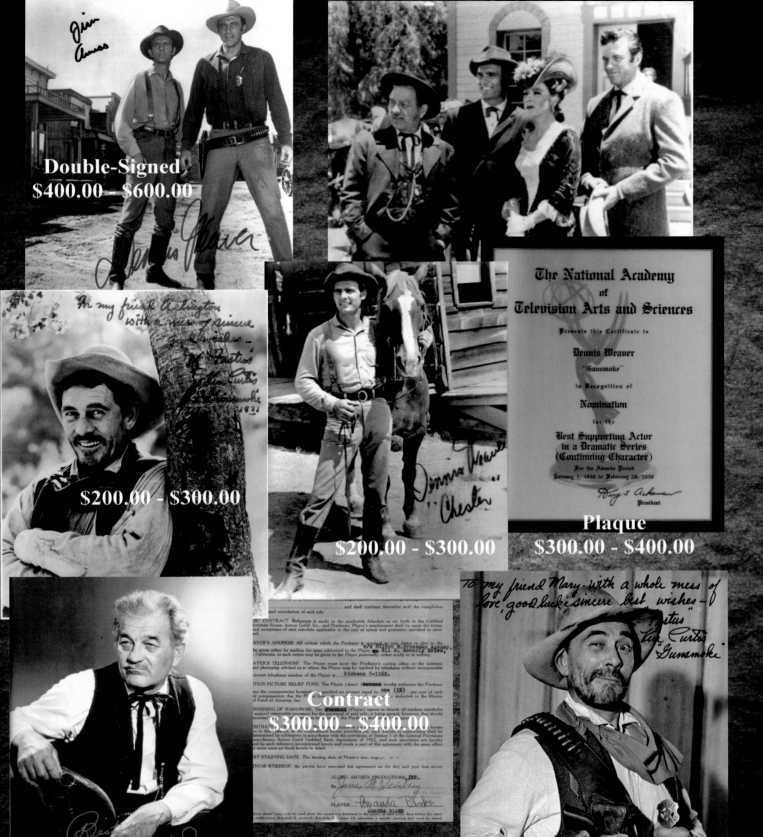

**Double-Signed**
$400.00 – $600.00

$200.00 – $300.00

$200.00 – $300.00

**Plaque**
$300.00 – $400.00

**Contract**
$300.00 – $400.00

$200.00 – $300.00

$400.00 – $600.00

# Lorne Greene - "Bonanza"
## 1915-1987

*with all good wishes Lorne Greene "BEN"*

**Autographed Photo - Estimated Value - $400.00 - $600.00**

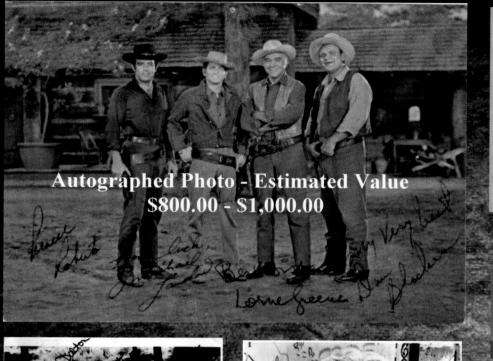

**Autographed Photo - Estimated Value**
**$800.00 - $1,000.00**

**4- Signature Clip**
**$600.00 - $800.00**

**$300.00 - $500.00**

**$200.00 - $300.00**

**$200.00 - $300.00**

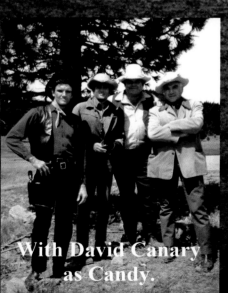

**With David Canary as Candy.**

**$400.00 - $600.00**

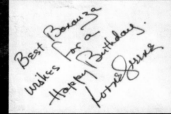

**$300.00 - $500.00**

# James Garner - "*Maverick*"

Jack Kelly

With Roger Moore
and Robert Colbert.

**Autographed Photo (Garner) - Estimated Value - $300.00 - $400.00**
**Autographed Photo (Kelly) - Estimated Value - $200.00 - $300.00**

# The Thalians

P. O. BOX 749

HUGH O'BRIAN
PRESIDENT

MARGARET WHITING
VICE PRESIDENT

L. W. BROWN
EXECUTIVE VICE PRESIDENT

MARIE WINDSOR
CORRESPONDING SECRETARY

PHYLLIS HARRIS
RECORDING SECRETARY

JOHN A. GRIFFIN
TREASURER

——

DIRECTORS

GLORIA HALEY BR
MARSHALL A. EDS
JACK HALEY, JR.
RUTH Y. LEWIS
BEN MELZER
LARRY ROBERTS
GEORGE SCHLATTE
LEW SPENCE
TONY TRAVIS

——

ADVISORS

JIMMY DURANTE
BRIAN FOY
JACK HALEY, SR.
DON HARTMAN
HARRY KARL
MERVYN LEROY
FRANK SINATRA
DANNY THOMAS

Mr. Jimmy Starr
14501 Valley Vista
Sherman Oaks, California

Dear Jimmy:

...enti...
...occ...
...the...
...THALIANS.

...posed of members of the enter...
...arts, is dedica...
...gram with our p...
...rbed children...
...our staff would...
...ither Bill Cor...
...tee, or Marshal...
...liaison for the...

..., WEbster 8-30...
..., CRestview 6-95...

... in this matter...

Sincerely,

THE THALIANS

*Hugh O'Brian*

Hugh O'Brian
President

# Gene Barry - "*Bat Masterson*"
### 1919-2009

**Autographed Photo - Estimated Value - $300.00 - $400.00**

342

# Fess Parker *1924-2010*

© WALT DISNEY PRODUCTIONS
World Rights Reserved

WALT DISNEY presents
"WESTWARD HO THE WAGONS!"
STARRING
FESS PARKER   KATHLEEN CROWLEY   JEFF YORK
An all - live action feature in
CinemaScope - Technicolor
Distributed by Buena Vista Film Distribution Co. Inc.

57/9

PERMISSION IS HEREBY GRANTED TO MAGAZINES
AND NEWSPAPERS TO REPRODUCE THIS PICTURE
ON CONDITION THAT IT IS ACCOMPANIED BY
THE COPYRIGHT NOTICE "© WALT DISNEY PRO-
DUCTIONS."

PRINTED IN U.S.A.

WH-1531

## DAVY CROCKETT, KING OF THE WILD FRONTIER

Fess Parker and Buddy Ebsen

## DANIEL BOONE

**Autographed Photo - Estimated Value - $300.00 - $400.00**

# Clint Walker - "*Cheyenne*"

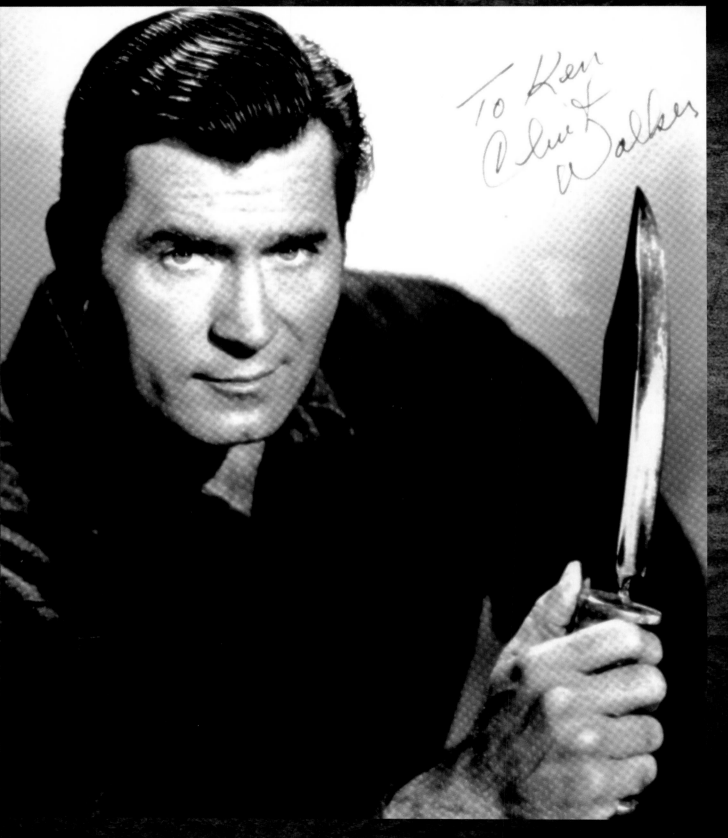

**Autographed Photo - Estimated Value - $300.00 - $400.00**

344

Clint Walker congratulating the Author Ken Owens
on winning first prize at Portland, Oregon
for western memorobilia displayed
behind them.

**Ty Hardin**

**Will Hutchins**

Clint Walker in contract dispute convinced studio
to hire Ty Hardin as Bronco Lane and Will Hutchins
as Sugarfoot in the *"Cheyenne"* T.V. series to
lessen his work load.

# Dale Robertson - "*Tales of Wells Fargo*"

Autographed Photo - Estimated Value - $300.00 - $400.00

# Clayton Moore - "The Lone Ranger"
## 1914-1999

**Autographed Photo (Moore) - Estimated Value - $400.00 - $600.00**
**Autographed Photo (Silverheels) - Estimated Value - $800.00 - $1,000.00**

THE LONE RANGER CREED

"I believe that to have a friend, a man must be one.

That all men are created equal and that everyone has within himself the power to make this a better world.

That God put the firewood there but that every man must gather and light it himself.

In being prepared physically, mentally, and morally to fight when necessary for that which is right.

That a man should make the most of what equipment he has.

That 'This government, of the people, by the people and for the people' shall live always.

That men should live by the rule of what is best for the greatest number.

That sooner or later...somewhere...somehow...we must settle with the world and make payment for what we have taken.

That all things change but truth, and that truth alone, lives on forever.

In my Creator, my country, my fellow man."

John Hart    The Lone Ranger and Silver

Brace
Beamer (radio)

Klinton Spillsbury & Michael Horse
in "*The Legend of the Lone Ranger*"

**Autographed Photo (Hart) - Estimated Value - $300.00 - $400.00**
**Autographed Creed (2 signatures) - Estimated Value - $400.00 - $600.00**

349

# Jock Mahoney - *"The Range Rider"*
## 1919-1989

*"Yancy Derringer"*

X. Brands, Frances Bergen and Jock Mahoney

Jock Mahoney and Dick Jones

**Double Autographed Photo - Estimated Value - $300.00 - $500.00**

# Hopalong Cassidy
## 1895-1972

To Kay
Good Luck
Hoppy

Jimmy Ellison

Russell Hayden

Rand Brooks

To Larry —
Wishing you happiness
Rand Brooks
"Lucky"

**Autographed Photo (Hoppy) - Estimated Value - $600.00 - $800.00**
**Autographed Photo (Brooks) - Estimated Value - $200.00 - $300.00**

351

# John Russell - "*Lawman*"
## *1921-1991*

**Double Autographed Photo - Estimated Value - $400.00 - $600.00**

Peter Brown, Peggie Castle and John Russell

**Autographed Photo - Estimated Value - $200.00 - $300.00**

# Peter Graves - "*Fury*"
## 1926-2010

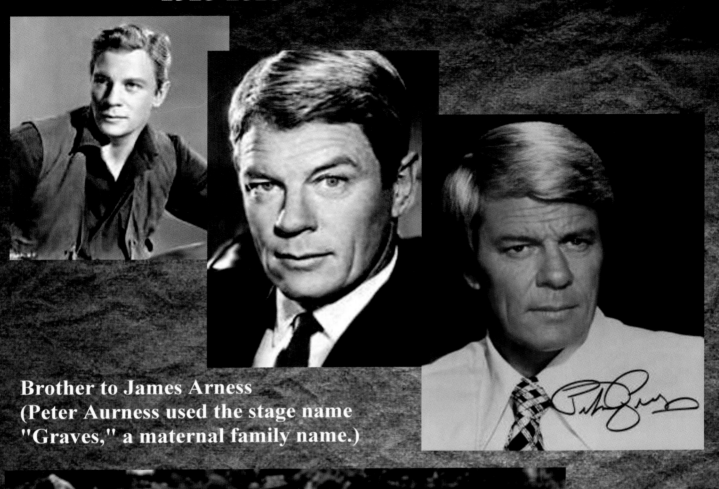

**Brother to James Arness
(Peter Aurness used the stage name
"Graves," a maternal family name.)**

**With William Fawcett and Bobby Diamond**

**Autographed Photo - Estimated Value - $200.00 - $300.00**

# James Drury - "*The Virginian*"

**Double Autographed Photo**
**$300.00 - $500.00**

**$400.00 - $600.00**

**$200.00 - $400.00**

**$200.00 - $300.00**

THE VIRGINIAN · THE VIRGINIAN · THE VIRGINIAN · THE VIRGINIAN · THE VIRGINIAN

**(5) Clip Signatures - Estimated Value - $300.00 - $500.00**

354

# Robert Horton - "*Wagon Train*"

**Autographed Photos - Estimated Value - $200.00 - $300.00**
**Double Clip Signature - Estimated Value - $400.00 - $600.00**

# THE DUKE

# Chapter Sixteen
## 1928-1978 John Wayne Westerns

# John Wayne 1907-1979

**1940 Autographed Photo - Estimated Value - $700.00 - $900.00**

**Autographed Photo - Estimated Value - $900.00 - $1,100.00**

May 1, 1953

Dear Jimmy:

We are proud that "The High and The Mighty,"
Ernest K. Gann's new novel was selected as the
Book Of the Month's May Selection. We are even
more proud to announce that we have acquired
the film rights to this book and will produce
it for Warner Brothers. William A. Wellman,
who just completed the motion picture "Island
In The Sky," another novel by Mr. Gann, will
direct "The High and The Mighty" when it goes
into production in the Fall.

No amount of fancy phrases could tell you as
much about "The High and The Mighty" as you will
provide for yourself after you read this book.
Hence, please accept the enclosed copy with our
sincerest compliments.

Very sincerely,

JOHN WAYNE

ROBERT FELLOWS

**Signed Letter With Sheet Music - Estimated Value - $1,200.00 - $1,500.00**

# 1930 - "*The Big Trail*"

With Martguerite Churchill

# 1931 - "*Range Feud*"

With Buck Jones

# 1933 - "*Riders of Destiny*"

# 1933 - "*Pals of the Saddle*"

The 3 Mesquiteers

# 1939 - "*Stagecoach*"

# 1966 - "*Stagecoach*"

THESE WERE THE TEN WHO FOUGHT INDIANS, OUTLAWS AND EACH OTHER AS THEY RODE TO GREATNESS ON THE STAGECOACH TO CHEYENNE!

A Martin Rackin Production

# STAGECOACH

CinemaScope · Color by DeLuxe

ANN-MARGRET · RED BUTTONS · MICHAEL CONNORS · ALEX CORD · BING CROSBY
BOB CUMMINGS · VAN HEFLIN · SLIM PICKENS · STEFANIE POWERS · KEENAN WYNN
MARTIN RACKIN · GORDON DOUGLAS · JOSEPH LANDON · DUDLEY NICHOLS
FROM A STORY BY ERNEST HAYCOX

# 1941 - "*Shepherd of the Hills*"

# 1942 - "*The Spoilers*"

1945 - "*Dakota*"

# 1947 - "Angel and the Badman"

# 1948 - "Red River"

RED RIVER

# 1949 - "*She Wore a Yellow Ribbon*"

# 1950 - "*Rio Grande*"

# 1956 - "*The Searchers*"

# 1959 - "*Rio Bravo*"

# 1960 - "*The Alamo*"

# 1960 - "*North to Alaska*"

# 1961 - "*Comancheros*"

# 1962 - "*...Liberty Vallance*"

# 1965 - "The Sons of Katie Elder"

# 1967 - "War Wagon"

# 1967 - "El Dorado"

# 1969 - "*True Grit*"

# 1969 - "*Undefeated*"

# 1970 - "Chisum"

# 1971 - "Big Jake"

# 1972 - "*The Cowboys*"

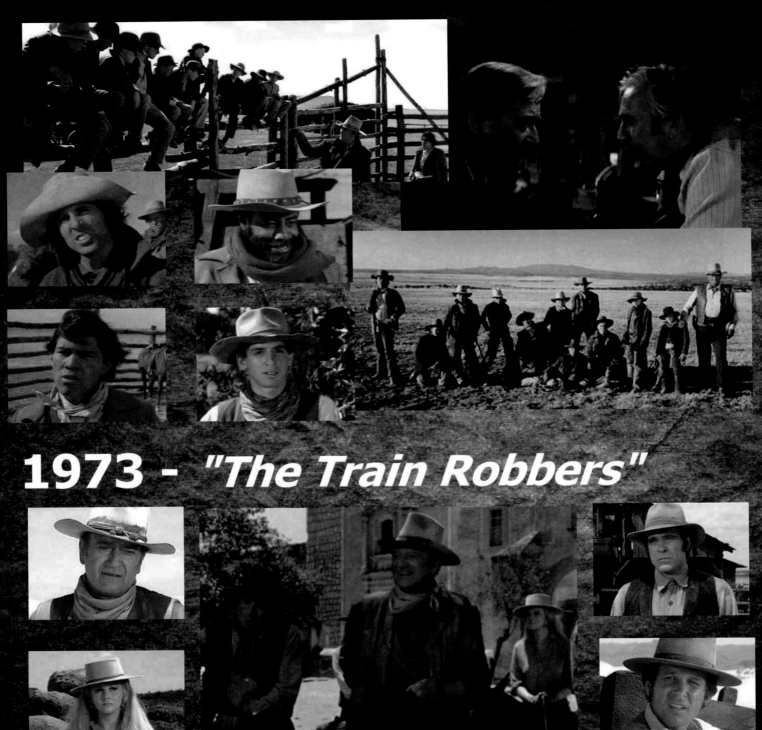

# 1973 - "*The Train Robbers*"

# 1973 - "Cahill US Marshal"

# 1975 - "Rooster Cogburn"

# 1976 - "*The Shootist*"

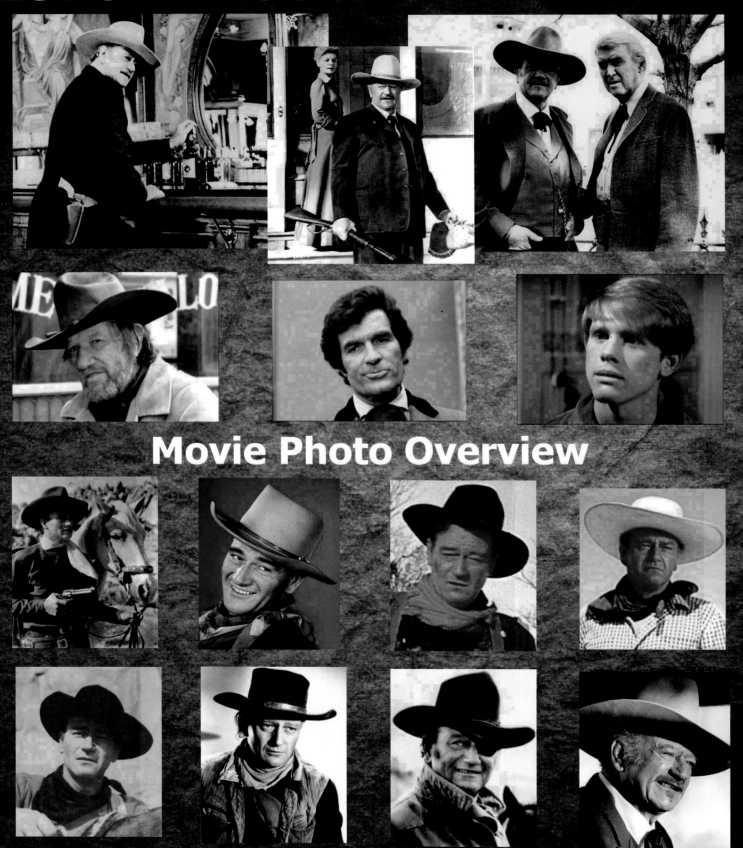

## Movie Photo Overview

John Wayne Movies (1928-1978) 44 Westerns - 150 Total Films.

# The Ford/Wayne Road/Stock Co.

John Ford

John Wayne

Harry Carey

Ward Bond

George O'Brien

Victor McLaglen

Ben Johnson

Bruce Cabot

Patrick Wayne

Grant Withers

Maureen O'Hara

Mildred Natwick

Hank Worden

Yakima Canutt

John Qualen

Chuck Roberson

Jack Pennick

Francis Ford

Paul Fix

Harry Carey Jr.

Originally small, tightly-knit band of he-men, hard drinkers and gamblers, united by affection and respect for John Ford and each other. They Spent 20 hour days in desolate locations and lived the lives they portrayed. John Ford was the force that brought them together, his and John Wayne's films kept them together.

# Chapter Seventeen
## 1930's-1970's Other Western Stars

# Other "A" Western Stars

**Gene Hackman**

**Tommy Lee Jones**

**Marlon Brando**

**Jack Nicholson**

**Dean Martin**

**Wayne Morris**

**Dennis Morgan**

**Ralph Meeker**

**Sterling Hayden**

**Wendell Corey**

**Cliff Robertson**

**Zachary Scott**

**Don Murray**

**Steve Forrest**

**Jack Lord**

**Monte Markham**

**Richard Arlen**

**(Wally Wales)
Hal Taliaferro**

**Richard Egan**

**Jeff Richards**

**If signed, Top Row Estimated Value - $400.00 - $600. 00
Next 3 Rows $200.00 - $400.00**

# Other Supporting Western Stars

Glen Corbett

Neville Brand

Dennis Hopper

Ernest Borgnine

Woody Strode

Guinn "Big Boy" Williams

Geoffrey Lewis

Arthur Hunnicutt

Hank Worden

Lon Chaney Jr.

Frank Lovejoy

Paul Richards

John Anderson

John Dehner

Earl Holliman

Tom London

Charles McGraw

Andrew Prine

Carleton Carpenter

Jerome Courtland

## If Signed, All Photos Estimated Value - $200.00 - $400.00

**Charles King**

**"Black" Jack O'Shea**

**Lane Bradford**

**Jack Lambert**

**Holly Bane**

**John Cason**

**Albert Dekker**

**Barton MacLane**

**Ted Decorsia**

**Fred Graham**

**Dan Duryea**

**Michael Pate**

**Henry Silva**

**Lyle Bettger**

**Gene Evans**

**Charles B. Middleton**

**Bill McKinney**

**Don Stroud**

**Dick Alexander**

**Pierce Lyden**

# If Signed, All Photos Estimated Value - $200.00 - $400.00

# Other Good / Bad Guys

Dennis Moore

Glenn Strange

J. Carrol Nash

William Bishop

Marshall Reed

House Peters Jr.

Grant Withers

L. Q. Jones

Jack Palance

Douglas Kennedy

Myron Healey

Bud Osborn

Henry Brandon

Steve Brodie

James Gregory

Edward Binns

R. G. Armstrong

Anthony Zerbe

Jeff Morrow

Vic Morrow

## If Signed, All Photos Estimated Value - $200.00 - $400.00

# Other Women in Westerns

**Ruth Mix**     **Jennifer Holt**     **Gail Russell**     **Linda Sterling**     **Fay McKenzie**

**Shirley Patterson**     **Marguerite Chapman**     **Anne Jeffreys**     **Frances Dee**     **Vera Ralston**

**Ona Munson**     **Shelly Winters**     **Dale Evans**     **Gale Davis**     **Olive Carey**

**Martha Hyer**     **Nell O'Day**     **Mary Murphy**     **Katherine Ross**     **Linda Evans**

**If Signed, All Photos Estimated Value - $200.00 - $400.00**

# Other T.V. Western Show Casts

**Rawhide**

**Restless Gun**

**Wanted Dead or Alive**

**Wild Wild West**

**Zoro**

**Broken Arrow**

**Death Valley Days**

**Guns of Will Sonnet**

**How the West Was Won**

**Lancer**

**Laramie**

**The Rebel**

**Sky King**

**Laredo**

**The Dakotas**

**Hawkeye**

**Hondo**
Ralph Tager

**Nakia**
Robert Forster

**Brave Eagle**
Keith Larsen

**The Adventures of Kit Carson**

## If Signed, All Photos Estimated Value - $200.00 - $400.00

| Reb Russell | Bill Cody | Steve Clark | Chubby Johnson | Gordon Jones |

| Harry Lauter | Ed Lauter | Wilford Brimley | Richard Farnsworth | Douglas V. Fowley |

| Kenne Duncan | Fredric Forrest | Rex Reason & Rhodes Reason | Robert Loggia | Jason Evers |

| Ed Faulkner | Cliff Lyons | Dave Sharpe | Dean Smith | Clint Ritchie |

If Signed, All Photos Estimated Value - $200.00 - $400.00

# Red Ryder & Little Beaver

**Garment Tag**

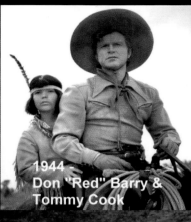

**1944 -
Don "Red" Barry &
Tommy Cook**

**Daisy Air Rifles - The Golden Years**

*Limited Edition of 500 Signed and Numbered*

*Fine Art Silk Screened Serigraph Print Full 23"x31"*

**Only $95.00 plus ship & postage.**

**Artist John W. Hampton**

**Jim Bannon & Don Kay Reynolds**

**1946-
Bill Elliot & Bobby Blake**

**1949-
Allan "Rocky" Lane & Bobby Blake**

**Artist
Fred Harmon**

# The Virginian

## "THE VIRGINIAN"

1902 - OWEN WISTER - (PLOT) THE VIRGINIAN, FALLING IN LOVE W/ MOLLY WOODS, A SCHOOL TEACHER, FROM THE EAST. SHE REJECTS HIM WHEN HE LEADS POSSE TO CATTLE RUSTLERS, HANGING STEVE, HIS FRIEND. WHEN WOUNDED, TRAILING TRAMPAS, MOLLY NURSES HIM BACK TO HEALTH. REJECTING HIM AGAIN, WHEN FACING TRAMPAS IN GUNGIGHT. BROUGHT TOGETHER IN THE END WHEN TRAMPAS IS DEAD.

1904 - (STAGE PLAY) DUSTIN FARNUM

1907-08-(STAGE PLAY) WM. S. HART. (TOLD WISTER SHOULD SHOW LOYALTY INSTEAD OF ABSTRACT NOTION OF JUSTICE.)

1918 - (PHOTOPLAY) DUSTIN FARNUM PROD. BY JESSE L. LASKY; DIR. BY CECIL B. DE MILLE.

1925 - (PHOTOPLAY) B.P. SCHULBERG(IND.)KEN HARLAN & FLORENCE VIDOR.

1929 - GARY COOPER - (SCHULBERG W/ PARAMOUNT).W/ MARY BRIAN AS MOLLY; RICHARD ARLEN AS STEVE; & WALTER HOUSTON AS TRAMPAS. RANDOLPH SCOTT ALSO APPEARED. VICTOR FLEMING DIRECTED. THE FILM MADE GARY COOPER A STAR.

1946 - JOEL MC CREA - AS " THE VIRGINIAN"; BARBARA BRITTON AS MOLLY; SONNY TUFFS AS STEVE; AND BRIAN DONLEVY AS TRAMPAS.

1962-71-(T.V.)- JAMES DRURY AS "THE VIRGINIAN", DOUG MC CLURE AS TRAMPAS (NICER THAN THE MOVIE VERSIONS), AND GARY CLARKE AS STEVE. LEE J. COBB & ROBERTA SHORE). 225 - 90 MIN. COLOR EPISODES WERE AIRED.

**Dustin Farnum "The Virginian"**

# The Cisco Kid

Warner Baxter

With Edmund Lowe

"CISCO KID"

1904 - O. HENRY - (SHORT STORY) THE CABALLERO'S WAY (ROBIN HOOD OF THE WEST, ILL-TEMPERED).

1914 - (ONE-REELER) SAME TITLE.

1919 - (UNIVERSAL)-2-REELER, THE BORDER TERROR

1929 - ( FOX ) - RAOUL WALSH, IN OLD ARIZONA, WARNER BAXTER STARRED AND WON OSCAR.

1931 - ( FOX ) - "THE CISCO KID" - EDMUND LOWE AS TEXAS RANGER AGAIN.

1939 - (20TH.-FOX)-"THE RETURN OF THE CISCO KID" ( BAXTER'S LAST CISCO)- CESAR ROMERO HAS PART AS "LOPEZ" W/ CRIS PIN MARTIN COMIC

1939 - (20TH-FOX)-CESAR ROMERO "CISCO KID & LADY" W/CRIS PIN MARTIN . (W.W.2, NO CISCO FILMS). (SIX CISCO FILMS MADE W/ CESAR ROMERO).

1944 - JAMES S. BURKETT & PHILLIP N. KRASNE GOT FOX'S "CISCO KID" (MONOGRAM). WANTED DUNCAN RENALDO AS CISCO.

1945 - "THE CISCO KID RETURNS"; "C.K. IN OLD N.M."; & "SOUTH OF THE RIO GRANDE" THREE WITH RENALDO AS CISCO. MARTIN GARRALAGA, A MEX. OPERA SINGER, PLAYS PANCHO. DUNCAN DIDN'T PLAY CISCO AS KILLER AND TERRORIST (INVOLVED IN GOVT. WORK, DROPPED FROM SERIES. SCOTT R. DUNLAP TOOK OVER PROD.

1946 - GILBERT ROLAND - "GAY CAVALIER"; "BEAUTY AND BANDIT"(3 MOVIES). HE PLAYED PART AS MEX. KILLER & TERRORIST. LAST FILM WAS, "KING OF BANDITS". 3 MORE FILMS ( 1947) AT REDUCED BUDGET.(LOST LATIN MARKET).

1948 - KRASNE,BOUGHT CISCO (3 ENTRIES, DROPPED).

1950 - FREDERIC ZIV(HEAD),KRASNE(PRODUCER),U.A. RENALDO(ASSOC. PROD.)& STAR.LEO CARILLO AS PANCHO (5 FEATURES) " GIRL FROM SAN L"

1950-56 -176 HALF HOUR T.V.SHOWS. 1990 TURNER T.V.

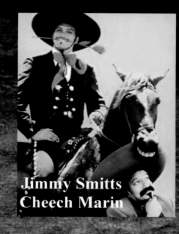

Jimmy Smitts
Cheech Marin

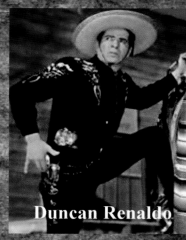

Duncan Renaldo

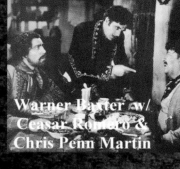

Warner Baxter w/ Ceasar Romero & Chris Penn Martin

Duncan Renaldo

Martin Garralaga

Duncan Renaldo w/ Leo Carrillo

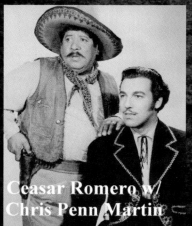

Ceasar Romero w/ Chris Penn Martin

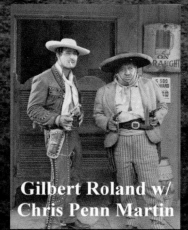

Gilbert Roland w/ Chris Penn Martin

**(8) Clip Signatures - Estimated Value - $400.00 - $600.00**

# The Big Country

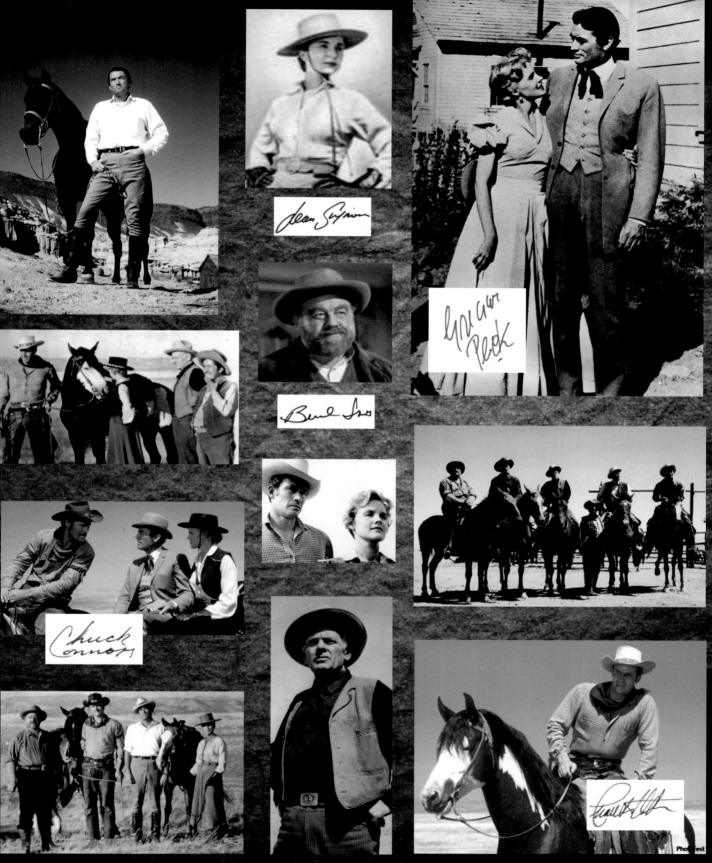

Jean Simmons

Gregor Peck

Burl Ives

Chuck Connors

**(5) Clip Signatures - Estimated Value - $400.00 - $600.00**

# Tombstone

BILL PAXTON

DANA DELANEY

POWERS BOOTHE

MICHAEL BEIHN

STEPHEN LANG

THOMAS H. CHURCH

JASON PRIESTLY

DANA NICHOLSON

**(4) Autographed Photo - Estimated Value - $800.00 - $1,000.00**

# The Magnificent Seven

**(5) Clip Signatures - Estimated Value - $400.00 - $600.00**

# onesome Dove

# Dances With Wolves

375 NORTH CAROLWOOD DRIVE
LOS ANGELES, CALIFORNIA 90077

March 2, 1992

Mr. Ken Owens
322 E. Johnston
Hemet, CA  92343

Dear Mr. Owens,

Thank you for your letter of
February 6th.

Mr. Peck says that your buckle
might be the one he wore.  He
didn't keep it after the movie.

Sincerely,

Victoria Haupenthal

Victoria Haupenthal
Executive Assistant to
Gregory Peck

# The Outlaw Josey Wales

# Bandolero

# Bite the Bullet

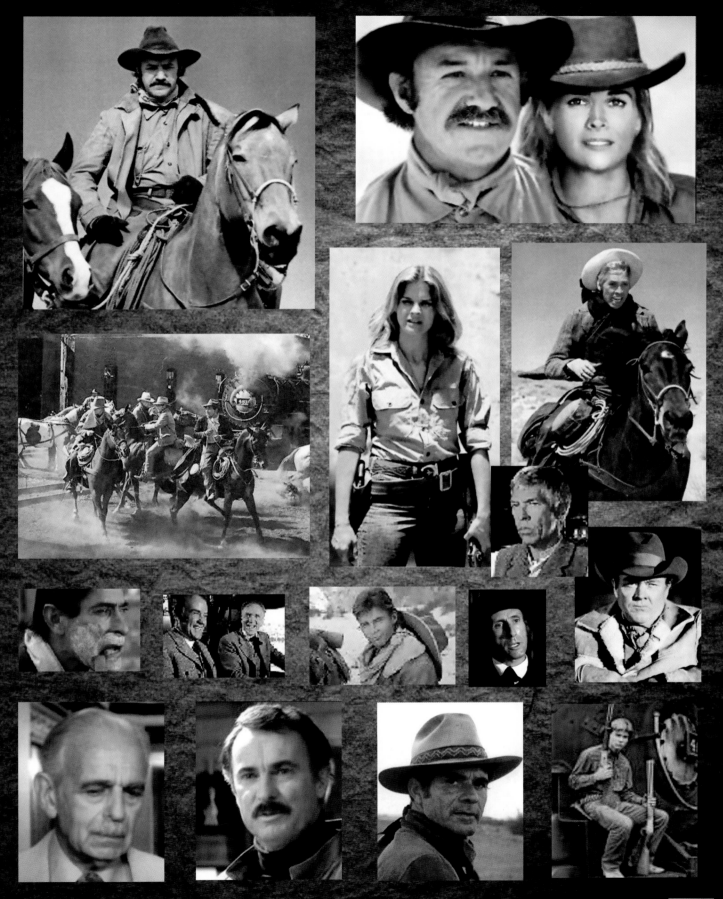

SEE HOW THE WEST WAS **FUN!**...

THE MIRISCH CORPORATION presents

**BURT LANCASTER** **LEE REMICK**

**JIM HUTTON** **PAMELA TIFFIN**

in JOHN STURGES'
'THE HALLELUJAH TRAIL'

also starring **DONALD PLEASENCE** **BRIAN KEITH**

MARTIN LANDAU  Produced and Directed by JOHN STURGES  Screenplay by JOHN GAY  Based on the Novel by BILL GULICK

Filmed in **ULTRA PANAVISION**  A Mirisch-Kappa Production Presented in 70mm Super **TECHNICOLOR**  Released thru UNITED ARTISTS

# Legends of the Fall

# Chapter Eighteen
## Various Related Western Movie Images

# Republic Poster Signed

27 Autographs:
1- John Agar
2- Gene Autry
3- Lash LaRue
4- Sunset Carson
5- Ben Johnson
6- Steve Brodie
7- Monte Hale
8- Shirley Patterson
9- George O'Brien
10- Kirby Grant
11- Bob Livingston
12- Faye McKenzie
13- Forrest Tucker
14- Jane Frazee
15- Clayton Moore
16- Charles "Durango" Starrett
17- Bob Steele
18- Nell O'Day
19- Yakima Canutt
20- Fred Scott
21- Henry Brandon
22- Bob Allen
23- Slim Pickens
24- Rod Cameron
25- Jennifer Holt
26- Gail Davis
27- Roy Rogers

**Autographed Photo - Estimated Value - $3,000.00 - $4,000.00**

**(2) Autographed Photos - Estimated Value - $400.00 - $600.00**

ous

Jack Oakie

MANY THANKS FOR YOUR KIND INTEREST, RUSTY.
'TIS PEOPLE LIKE YOU WHO MAKE AN ACTOR'S
WORK SEEM WORTHWHILE —
LUCK, LOVE, LAUGHS AND LONG LIFE TO
YOU AND YOURS.
BEST, ALWAYS, IN ALL WAYS —
01 OCTOBER, 1982
MYRON
HEALEY

Clip Signatures - Estimated Value - $50.00 - $100.00 ea.

# Jennifer Jones

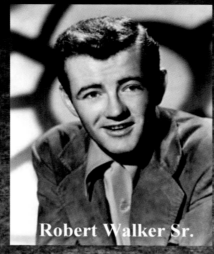
Robert Walker Sr.

Jr.

Jennifer Jones was born Phyllis Isley in Oklahoma. She was made a member of the Pawnee indian tribe there. She appeared in some 'B' westerns. She married Robert Walker. Robert Walker Jr. is their son. David O. Selznick later produced "Duel in the Sun", married her and changed her name to Jennifer Jones. She had an award winning career with movies like "Song of Bernadette". Her last movie was "The Towering Inferno". She later married Norton Simon of art museum fame on Colorado Blvd. accross from the Rose Bowl in Passadena, Ca. She adequately ran that museum for the remainder of her life.

Davis O. Selznick

As Phyllis Isley

1997 lifetime achievement award.

Norton Simon Museum

# Royal Canadian Mounted Police
## In Movies and Television

With Gary Cooper.

With Alan Ladd.

2 Versions of *"Rose Marie"*

N.W Mounted Police

Richard Simmons in
T.V.'s Seargent Preston
with Yukon King

William S. Hart

Candian Mounted Police.

# John Wayne Studios

## John Wayne
50 yrs. of movies - 150 movies - 44 westerns - 14 w/ John Ford
(Father of 7 children - Grandfather of 23)

**Studios he worked for and with in his career:**

1926-1931 - Fox years

1931-1932 - Columbia

1932-1933 - Mascot Serials (Poverty Row

1932-1933 - Warner Brothers

1933-1935 - Monogram (Lone Star Years)

1935-1936 - Republic (Monogram, Lone Star & Mascot merged)

1936-1937 - Six for Universal

Oscar *"True Grit"* 1969

1938-1939 - Republic (Three Mesquiteeers)

    1939 - Stagecoach (John Ford, Argosy)

1939-1940 -RKO Radio Pictures (Back to Republic)

    1940 -Universal and Paramount (Cecil B. DeMille & John Ford)

    1944 -RKO and Republic.

    1951 -Warner Bros. (John Ford & Wayne-Fellows Productions)

1960's-70's -Batjac (John Wayne's company). Managed by Michael Wayne.

(Affiliated with other companies also during his last 20 years.)

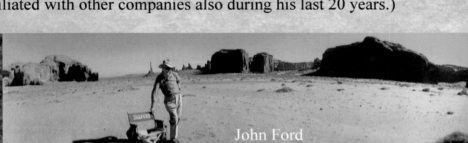

John Ford

# Country-Western Singers

"Legend of the Lone Ranger"

"Poncho and Lefty"

"Barbarosa"

Dukes of Hazzard

Movie "Your Cheatin' Heart" - Soundtrack Hank Williams Jr.

Drifting Cowboys

Ernest Tubb

1940's Westerns

Riders in the Sky

Eddie Arnold

Vaughn Monroe

Ghost Riders
in the Sky.

Burl Ives

The Oak Ridge Boys

The Statlers

Whatever happened
to Randolph Scott?

# Worth Mentioning -Dvd's

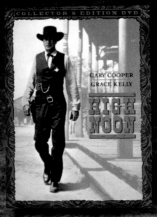

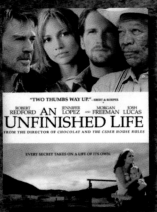

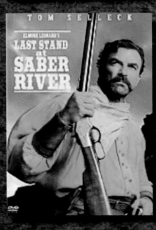
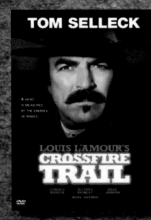
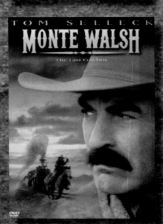
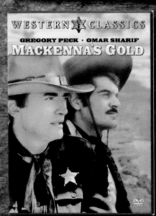

**Two Lobby Cards of Hopalong Cassidy and John Wayne - $100.00 - $200.00 ea.**

**Nick Adams signed $2-400.00**

**Dick Foran**

*"Johnny Guitar"*

**Joan Crawford and Sterling Hayden.**

**Ken Owens**

**Joe Beeeler, western artist.**

PETER SHERAYKO AND OSO

**At Old Trail Town Cody, Wyo.**

**1896-1987**

J.K.Ralston original Painting (1911)

Hangman
Maledon

Ben Dalton        Judge
Frank Dalton      Isaac C. Parker

**Judge Isaac Parker- For 21 years (1875-1896) Judge of U.S. Court of western district of Arkansas was the law west of Fort Smith holding exclusive jurisdiction over 74,000 sq. miles and 60,000 people in Arkansas and Indian territory. 200 deputy U.S. Marshals carried out 79 hangings. (Daltons at R. brothers to outlaws killed in Coffeeville, Kansas.)**

**Frank Dalton was killed serving an arrest warrant in Choctaw Bottoms.**

# Worth Mentioning

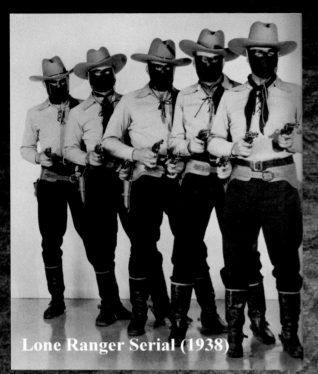

**Lone Ranger Serial (1938)**

L.toR.: Lee Powell, George Letz (aka George Montgomery), Hal Taliaferro (aka Wally Wales), Lane Chandler and Herman Brix (aka Bruce Bennett)

Thermopolis, Wyoming's Tim McCoy's interest in Indians, like William S. Hart, transported 100's of Indians to Hollywood for Western movies.

Ralston Purina's souvenir signed Tom Mix photo. Estimated Value $4 - 600.00

**John Wayne elected mayor of Encino, California from Spade Cooley.**

**Leo Carrillo pictured with Don
and Don with letter to both.**

**Pat Buttram Emcee at Beverly Hilton
with John Wayne and Ronald Reagan.**

**Irish/Cherokee Connection:**
Connections in the entertainment field.

Heretofore, other minorities have gained their place in the entertainment field. It's time the Irish/Cherokee connection was noticed. This also includes other American Indians. Below are only a few of many. Willie, Merle, Waylon, Glen Ford and Gregory Peck and others might fall into this category. If you know, speak up.

Irish/Cherokee

Elvis Presley    Johnny Cash    James Garner    Loretta Lynn    Crystal Gayle    Rita Cooliddge

Choctaw                                          Cherokee

Roy Rogers    Johnny Bench    Burt Reynolds    Cher    Tim McGraw    Gordon Lightfoot

# Other Movies, Stars and Casts

*"Silverado"*

**Butch and Sundance**

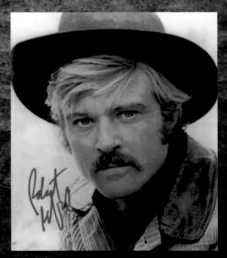

**Autographed Photos - Estimated Value - $300.00 - $500.00 each**

**John Lupton**  **H.M. Wynant**  **Jan Merlin**  **Wally West**

**Wayde Preston**  **Richard Martin**  **Jon Hall**  **Lane Chandler**

**Laurence Tierney**  **Leo Carrillo**  **Omar Sharif**  **Montie Montana**

**Will Hutchins**  **Nick Adams**  **Dick Jones**  **Ben Cooper**

# Autographed Photos - Estimated Value - $200.00 - $400.00 ea.

# Other Movies, Stars and Casts

Rod Taylor

Jeff Chandler

Brian Keith

Woody Strode

Sterling Holloway

J.C. Flippin at R. with Jimmy Stewart and Walter Brennan.

Steve Pendleton

*"Little House"*

*"3:10 to Yuma"*
Van Heflin and Glen Ford.

Morgan Freeman

Lee Roberts

Don Haggerty

Jason Robards

Jackie Cooper

## All Photos If Signed - Estimated Value $200.00 - $400.00

Strother Martin

Jeff Corey

Jim Corey

Bruce Dern

Dick Foran

Don Coleman

3 Photos From "Vengance Valley" Lancaster's first Western.

**Autographed Photos - Estimated Value - $200.00 - $400.00 ea.**

# Other Movies, Stars and Casts

"Five Card Stud"

"River of No Return"

THE CULPEPPER CATTLE CO.

"Monte Walsh"

"Fort Apache"

"The Oxbow Incident"

"The Oklahoma Kid"

Humphrey Bogart and James Cagney

T.V.'s "The Yellow Rose"

Movie stars touring to promote
Erroll Flynn's first western *"Dodge City"*

Entire cast & crew from Andy Devine Movie

WANTED

"Young Riders" with Josh Brolin
& Stephen Baldwin

This is Your Life
with Roy Rogers

John Wayne commercial with TV stars

# Gallery of Color Photos

# Gallery of Color Photos

# Gallery of Color Photos

# Behind the Scenes & Posed Photos

*"Johnny Guitar"*

*"Little Big Man"*

John Wayne's *"Alamo"*

Buster Keaton

John Ford in Monument Valley

Tim McCoy

*"Cat Ballou"* Jane Fonda with 3 different Lee Marvin characters.

Morris Ankrum

Trevor Bardette

James Griffith

Royal Dano

Sometimes confused by the author one for the other.

# Photo Collage of Western Stars

(10 of the sexiest women in westerns.)

# Post 1990 Western Movies

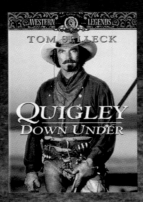

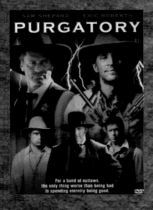

The above post-1990 movies prove the western genre is still alive. The efforts by Clint Eastwood, Kevin Costner, Sam Elliott, Tom Selleck, Robert Duval, Tommy Lee Jones make it so. Later movies by Liam Neeson, Pierce Brosnan, Russell Crowe, Christian Bale and Brad Pitt, who are known for other genres, the western will continue in theatres and on television.

# Western Movie Locations

Monument Valley

Beals's Cut - Newhall, Ca.

Vasquez Rocks

Oak Creek Canyon

Old Tucson

Old Tucson

Universal Sound Stage

Gene Autry at Melody Ranch

Lone Pine, Bishop Ca.
Alabama Hills (inset)

Kanab, Utah

Paramount Studios

Warner Ranch

Warner Brothers

# Rodeo Stars - Western Movie Connection

Casey Tibbs

Jackson Sundown

World Champion Cowboy Larry Mahan. Compliments of Texas Ford Dealers.
Larry Mahan

Yakima Canutt (3)

Jim Shoulders (2)

Ben Johnson

Will James

Hoot Gibson

Lane Frost

Tuff Hedeman

(2) Jack Williams, horsefall in *"Tonka"* western movie extra and singer.

# Western Movie/T.V. Merchandise

Over the years the Author collected many items belonging to western movie stars. He met many of them such as Clint Walker above. This helped create the interest in Western memorabilia & autographs. Thus the reason for writing this book. Among items pictured above are: Buck Jones' hat, chaps and gunbelt. Tom Mix engraved gun and many other items as you can see. Below are 3 autographed hats from Roy Rogers, Gene Autry and Rex Allen.

**Tom Mix**

**w/ Burt Reynolds**

4 frames above show items bought mostly from radio and t.v. shows such as Hopalong Cassidy, Roy Rogers, Gene Autry, The Lone Ranger, Red Ryder and others.

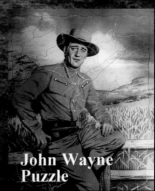

**John Wayne Puzzle**

2 matted frames are examples of well displayed photos and clip signatures.

# John Wayne & Family

First wife Josephine Saenz

Second wife Esperanza Baur

Third Wife Pilar Pallete

Michael Wayne

Patrick Wayne

*Patrick Wayne*

John Ethan

*"Hondo"*

**Marisa Wayne**

John Ethan, Patrick and Michael Wayne -Melinda Munoz, Toni LaCava and Aissa Wayne

**JOHN WAYNE**

BATJAC PRODUCTIONS
1022 PALM AVENUE
HOLLYWOOD, CALIFORNIA

BATJAC

MICHAEL A. WAYNE

BATJAC PRODUCTIONS, INC.
9570 WILSHIRE BOULEVARD. SUITE 400
BEVERLY HILLS, CALIF. 90212          (213) 278-9870

# Vintage Stars in Westerns

Autographed Photos Above - Estimated Value - $800.00 - $1000.00
Merle Haggard - Estimated value - $200.00 - $400.00

# Equipment Providers to the Stars

**Ed Bohlin**        **Bob Brown**        **Nudie**        **Peter Sherayko**

Ed Bohlin- Silver saddle and gun rig maker to the stars.
Bob Brown- Leather Carver for Bohlin and many western stars.
Nudie- Western Clothesmaker to the stars (North Hollywood).
Peter Sherayko- (Caravan West Productions) Saddles, Gunrigs,
horses and riders for later westerns such as *"Tombstone"*.

# Authors/Directors - Books to Movies

*"Union Pacific"* by Zane Grey and Owen Wister's *"The Virginian"* as well as Louis L'Amour and Ernest Haycox, and other author's novels and short stories, are examples adapted into movies by directors such as Cecil B. De Mille, John Ford and others.

*"Union Pacific"*

Owen Wister

*"The Virginian"*

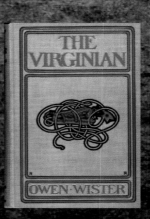

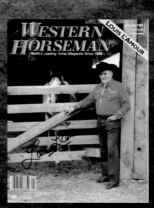

Autographed Letter (Zane Grey)  $400.00 - $600.00, Photo $300.00- $400.00, Clip $200.00 - $300.00
Signed Check (Cecil B. De Mille)$4 - $600.00, Clip Signature and Union Pacific Token $2 - $400.00
John Ford Clip Signature $200.00 - 400.00 - Louie L'Amour - Signed Photo $200.00 - 400.00

**"BAT" MASTERSON**

WILLIAM BARCLAY MASTERSON IN ... IN 1859. HE MOVED TO KANSAS. ...MI. A BUFFALO HUNTER, ...NG MEAT FOR THE RAILROADS. ...BE WALLS, TEX., JUNE ', 1874, HE ...LY DIXON WERE ATTACKED BY ...PARKER'S COMANCHES. IN 1875, ...RED FIRST MAN OVER WOMAN. ...ACK TO DODGE CITY, KANSAS, AS ...MARSHAL UNDER WYATT EARP ...SHERIFF, NOV. 6, 1877. IN 1878, ...ER, ED., A DEPUTY MARSHAL. WAS ...IN A DODGE CITY SHOOTOUT. ...MARSHAL. HE DEALT FARO IN ...LLE, COLO. IN TOMBSTONE, HE ...O WYATT EARP, AND LEFT BEFORE ...ORRAL, 1882. MARSHAL OF TRINIDAD, ...ADO. HE FOLLOWED BOOM TOWNS. ...IN DODGE CITY, RENO, LAS VEGAS, ...NVER, WHERE PROMOTING FIGHTS ...HEATER. HE MARRIED EMMA WALT... ...NOV. 21, 1891. IN 1896, SPORTS WRITER, ...VELT, EDITOR N.Y. PAPER, WROTE ...MNS. ACTIVE IN FIGHTING BUSINESS ...TO NEW YORK, 1902. APPOINTED ...Y.S. MARSHAL OF N.Y. BY TEDDY ...E COLUMNS UNTIL DEATH, OCT. 25, ...F HEART ATTACK.

**WYATT EARP**

1848 - 1929

LAWMAN - KAN.

TOMBSTONE, AZ.

O.K. CORRAL 1881

**FRANK JAMES**

1843 - 1915

QUANTRILL'S RAIDERS

JAMES YOUNGER GANG

1867 - 76

SURRENDERED 1882

CHAS. EMMERICH & CO.

FEATHERS,

RETURN TO

Department of Kansas, G. A. R.

MEMORIAL HALL

TOPEKA, KANSAS

...uthentic signatures of real west characters bring a premium. Few exist before 1900. After 1... ...hey exist as autographs. Matted Signatures of Bat Masterson, Wyatt Earp and Frank James... ...stimated at $4,000.00 - $5,000.00 each. Unmatted signatures of Pat Garrett, Emmett Dalton... ...ole Younger are estimated at $2,000.00 - $3,000.00 each. If matted would bring same value... ...bove. The same can be applied to western movie stars throughout the book. If matted they a... ...orth as much as signed pictures, letters etc. William F. Cody estimated at $1,000.00 - $1,20...

# Appendixes

"The Great Train Robbery"

William S. Hart

JAMES CRUZE
THE COVERED WAGON
a Paramount Picture

"The Covered Wagon"

J. Warren Kerrigan and Lois Wilson

"Iron Horse"

# Western Movie History

In the beginning, Edwin S. Porter (1890) happened into the fledgling motion picture industry by becoming a projectionist on the Edison Vitascope. In the late 1890s, trying to perfect the new projector, he became a professional photographer for news and scenic films sold to Vaudeville houses. The Edison Company became one of his best customers and he then became an employee there. He worked on a lightweight camera and became the first to devise "story" films. He developed film editing and special effects. Porter was the first to direct feature films in the U.S., and the first to use creative trick photography. All these new innovations heightened suspense and elevated Porter to chief producer for the Edison Company.

Gilbert M. Anderson (1902) applied at Edison's Studio. Porter hired him as a player for fifty cents an hour. Porter's The Great Train Robbery, thought to be his best film, was a result of a railroad company financing him to advertise the benefits of the railroad. The commercial impact was great, as Nickelodeons all over the country ran the film for two years, to capacity audiences. The Great Train Robbery was cinematic, with camera angles, editing, and parallel action without subtitles. George Barnes, as a desperado, appeared on screen and fired his gun directly at the audience. Women reportedly screamed and fainted.

D. W. Griffith worked for Porter at Edison's as an actor. He wanted to be a playwright, so he moved to Biograph where he became a director.

Carl Laemmle (1916-1936) did more for general western production than anyone else in the industry. He was from Germany, penniless, and non-English speaking. He was a promoter but over a dispute with owners he moved to Chicago, investing his savings in a Nickelodeon. He recognized the financial pluses of film exhibition. He had much success and invested in a second theater. Next, he started his own film exchange to insure the quality of the screen product. He became a millionaire.

A trust company took over Biograph Co. The Trust Co. included: Edison, The Selig Co., George K. Spoor of Essanay, others including French Pathé, etc. They formed the Motion Picture Patents Co. to curtail independent filmmaking. Laemmle sold ten percent of his company for $2,500.00 to Robert Cochrane and they formed the Motion Picture Co. of America (IMP). However, the Trust Co. had 10,000 theaters and became rich. They filed 300 lawsuits against Laemmle.

Porter, dissatisfied at Edison in the Trust Wars, in 1909 left to enter independent production. He founded Defender Picture Co. and he hired Arthur Miller, who became one of the best cinematographers of his time. Porter did one-reelers and released them weekly through Laemmle's IMP Co. They became business associates. By 1912, Laemmle, emerging from the lawsuits, introduced Porter to Adolph Zukor, who associated himself with the Loews theater chain. They founded Famous Players and Porter became production manager. He had offered the job to D. W. Griffith for $50,000.00 a year. Griffith declined, suggesting Porter. A decade later, when Zukor got Griffith, times had changed and both were like other pioneers that the maturing industry had left behind. Laemmle survived and let Porter go back to Zukor for a lack of productivity and imagination.

From Famous Players, Porter moved to the West Coast. Lasky Studios made some pictures including Mary Pickford. Porter left in 1915 and tinkered with technical innovations and problems. Porter died in New York City in 1941. He seldom went to movies. He said he lost "the initiative and excitement."

The innovations from The Great Train Robbery continued to influence later westerns. G. M. Anderson was convinced the future was in the production of moving pictures. He left Edison and went to Vitagraph as director in 1904. Pittsburgh theater owners hired him to produce one and two-reeler films for them. He left and went to Chicago in 1907. Several companies were located there. Anderson persuaded William Selig to take the company to Colorado. Anderson intended to produce "cowboy" pictures in the tradition or spirit of The Great Train Robbery. Selig didn't go. Anderson returned to Chicago and partnered with George K. Spoor, a distributor of screen equipment, and moved to California. Selig followed then.

Spoor and Anderson's new company, Essanay, representing their initials with an Indian Head logo. Anderson now manufactured westerns on his own theories. Peter B. Kyne, a prolific writer for the screen, published a story on Broncho Billy. When Anderson read the story, he purchased the rights.

California offered what was needed for westerns, natural settings from deserts to mountains, lakes, forests, and plains. Anderson decided to star in the films as a good/bad guy, "Broncho Billy" Anderson. The first film was *Broncho Billy and the Baby* in 1915. He did one-reelers at first, then two-reelers, one a week at $800.00 each. He grossed up to $50,000.00. Continuous releases led to great success.

By 1912, Anderson earned up to $125,000.00 a year as producer, director, and western star. There were 375 short westerns made between 1908 and 1915. His westerns influenced many who followed the good/bad guy image. As William S. Hart was abandoning it, Tom Mix, Harry Carey, Buck Jones, Hoot Gibson, and George O'Brien were using it. Movies on down through the years used it. John Wayne, for example, used it in *Red River*, *The Searchers*, and *True Grit*. Many others did also. Requests for four and five reel films began, especially with the popularity of Charlie Chaplin and Stan Laurel comedies. Anderson went into production and then retirement. Thomas Ince and William S. Hart didn't cause it; changing times did.

By 1918, Essanay was about to go out of business, with other companies making better pictures and disputes with companies and Louis B. Mayer. Anderson did retire.

In 1903, Thomas Harper Ince was a brash, ambitious man in New York and did not like New York stage actor William S. Hart. The basic reason was that Hart was older than Ince. At 13, Ince promoted his own ailed stock company. Ince had acted in Vaudeville with Joseph Smiley, who now was well off and got Ince a job acting at IMP. Ince moved up to director from Biograph back to IMP. Ince needed Laemmle's approval and Ince bent his ear and got the job. Ince worked a lot with Mary Pickford and other film stars. He became an experienced producer/director.

In 1909, gaming was barred in New York. Two bookies, Kessel and Bauman, did not like what they believed to be Laemmle's incompetence, so they started Reliance Production and Bison Life Pictures in California. They wanted Ince to move from IMP to their company, and were interested in increasing his salary from $60.00 weekly to $150.00. Ince maneuvered, which proved unnecessary, as Kessel and Bauman were determined to give him the job. Ince made westerns and ran the Max Sennett films there too. He did not do so much indoor studio work.

Most westerns were haphazard, made up before or during shooting. Ince wanted to systematize productions and scenarios around plots, action sets, costumes, and dialogue put into the shooting, script writing, and filmmaking. All this was to be a collective enterprise. This was probably the beginning of the "Studio System." So, it is considered that Ince is probably most important to modern films at Griffith. Ince made his best film during this time, *The Birth of a Nation*.

Miller Brothers 101 Ranch Wild West Show wintered in Venice, California. Ince hired the whole show for $2500.00 a week. Now, for western films, Ince had it all: cowboys, Indians, cattle, buffalo, tepees, stagecoaches, and wagons. To produce westerns, Ince moved to 14,000 acres of land north of Santa Monica, California, known as "Inceville" in 1910. Ince made many westerns and he had a feeling for the Indians there, as William S. Hart had. Ince was not as creative as Griffith, but he was an organizer. He hired Francis Ford (John Ford's brother) away from Vitagraph in 1913. He was hired as an actor and director. Ford was independent and wanted control over Bison westerns. This suited Ince and freed him from doing everything himself. Ince, however, retained control of the "final cut." Ford did not like it but this made for better films. This period developed more actors, films, etc. Mary Pickford went from Laemmle to Griffith and back.

The Gish Sisters, Lillian and Dorothy, had seen a Pickford film and knew her. It was 1912. They went to Biograph in New York and Griffith gave them a screen test. Griffith was filming at the time with another newcomer, Harry Carey. Laemmle lost Pickford and Ince, Porter was a liability, and Laemmle got Mack Sennett on gambling debts. Sennett was broke, but Bison financed him in a comedy company. Sennett was surprised. His comedies were profitable, as were Ince's westerns. Laemmle needed talent for IMP. He tricked Kessel and Bauman at Bison with "breach of contract." They, in turn, raided IMP. Ince was nettled by this.

Grace Cunard, who had been encouraging Ford against Ince, prompted Ford to make his move. Ford got word to Laemmle that he, and not Ince, was reason for the success of Bison westerns. Laemmle got $17,000.00 in damages in his suit, and rights to use the Bison 101 trade mark and the services of Francis Ford as an actor/ director. Laemmle had a western unit at last and purchased Nestor Co. at Sunset and Gower in Hollywood (Gower Gulch), where later character actors and stuntmen waited on the corner daily to be picked up for movie parts. Kessel and Bauman at Bison were reeling, but still had Ince and Sennett.

# Western Movie History Continued

In 1912, William S. Hart, touring in Trail of the Lonesome Pine, made his first visit to Inceville and Ince, glad to see him, had Ann Little ride over and meet him. Her pinto horse reared and knocked Hart's cap off. This was Hart's first meeting with Fritz, the horse that would be his. Hart spoke to Ince of wanting to make westerns. Ince was not sure of the 42 year old's potential as a star. Hart had done westerns on stage in The Squaw Man (1904) and The Virginian (1906). He was touring for two years and that would give Ince time to think on the matter. In the end, Ince felt he was indebted to Hart for story orientations and real Sioux Indian's importation.

Art Acord was a fine horseman before he was in film. He met Hoot Gibson in a wild west show in 1910. Gibson was a world champion cowboy in 1912. Both were signed by D. W. Griffith as stuntmen. During 1921-22, Tom Mix, Hoot Gibson, and Art Acord's paths kept crossing, visiting at the 101 Ranch or working for Col. Selig. Francis Ford's natural acting contrasted with William S. Hart's melodramatic approach. Mutual substituted "Kay Bee" (Kessel and Bauman) for the Bison trademark. William S. Hart used the horse Midnight but 101 Miller Bros. would not sell. Hart then used and purchased Fritz from The N.Y. Motion Picture Co. Hart's westerns were like others of the teens, featuring crude attire and dusty streets of worn towns and ranches. But Hart's films were keenly romantic, sentimental, melodramatic, and some had ridiculous plots. Action was secondary to overstated, idealistic story lines. D. W. Griffith and the others mentioned previously all were in this early industry at about the same time from 1900 to the 1920s. In addition to the stars mentioned above, many other actors came in at this time of the silent '20s. So many short films were being made, all you had to do was be good looking and ride a horse. Many of these carried over into the talking "B" westerns of the 1930s. D. W. Griffith's The Birth of the Nation was a success but caused a Russian ban. Louis B. Mayer called Harry Aitken, who had helped Griffith with funds for Birth. Griffith moved The Majestic Film Co. to Epoch when the film was finished. Mayer wanted New England distribution rights. Mayer offered $50,000.00 and a 50/50 split after he got back the initial cost. Birth netted Mayer more than one million dollars.

Harry Sherman bought rights in 16 western states for $100,000.00. When Sherman came to New York, Aitken went to Epoch's bank on Wall Street to deposit the money. The Birth of a Nation influenced all later movies, especially westerns. Harry "Pop" Sherman was an asset to the western film industry for many years to come. Sherman bought up all interest and the bookies retired. Aitken, at La Junta, California, put Ince, D. W. Griffith, and Sennett under personal contract. These three directors were given salaries and stock options in Triangle Acting Co. Ince and Sennett spurred on and made their finest films. Griffith went forward making Intolerance, which failed. He drank. His brother, through annuities, kept him from going broke. In 1926, he said, pretty much on retiring, "Writers are the only ones who can express their egos. Directors can't. They have to satisfy everyone."

As the 1920s advanced, D. W.'s star tarnished. Zukor gave him $165,000.00 a year. He became more and more heartbroken. Zukor said, "He didn't fail, the procession passed him by." D. W. Griffith died in 1948 of a cerebral hemorrhage. Other companies were formed by different people. They came and went as the film industry grew, especially the westerns. The silent '20s turned into the talking "B" westerns of the 1930s and '40s, then the "A" westerns of the 1950s and '60s. Better effects and acting, along with evolving improvements, continued into the present.

O ne early film company was United Artists, 1919, founded by D. W. Griffith, Mary Pickford, Charles Chaplin, and Douglas Fairbanks, Sr. In the 1930s, however, all trails led to Republic, the studio that raised itself by its own bootstraps through wholesale commitment to the "B" western. Republic was started by Herbert J. Yates in 1935. The genre had faltered some at the end of the silent '20s and the early 1930s. Yates, who through his company, processed half of the released footage in America to independents on Poverty Row. Yates combined some of the other companies into Republic and, through the western, and along with Monogram, R.K.O., Lone Star, and others, revived the western with audiences, old and new, to attend new, improved westerns.

Let's not forget the serial. Serials were chaptered events that left viewers hanging each week to see what happened to the hero (cliff-hangers). The next week he usually came out okay, only to be in a fix the following week. Most Saturday afternoons were spent watching cartoons, the main feature and then a chapter of a serial to bring you back the next week.

Nat Levine was born in New York City in 1899. At the age of 13, Levine worked for the Marcus Loew theater chain. He worked his way up and moved his offices to Santa Monica Boulevard in Los Angeles, California, where he formed Mascot Pictures in 1927.

Since he began, Nat Levine completed a total of seven silent pictures, twenty-four sound serials, and nineteen features. Many stars were in these serials, including Gene Autry, Ken Maynard, and Tom Tyler. Nat Levine was the "King of the Serials." Loews became a part of M.G.M. with Louis B. Mayer. Fox became 20th Century Fox. Others were Paramount, Universal, and Warner Brothers, with its adult westerns for television in the 1950s and '60s.

The making of westerns continued through the mid-1970s. Now occasionally westerns appear and keep the genre alive, thanks to actors and directors like Clint Eastwood, Kevin Costner, Sam Elliott, and Tom Selleck.

Live long western movies!

**Founders
United Artists**

**Signed Photos - Estimated Value - $400.00 - $600.00**

# Western Movie History Visionaries

Thomas A. Edison

Edwin S. Porter

G.M. Anderson

D.W. Griffith

Carl Laenmle

Adolph Zucor

William Selig

Jessie L. Lasky

Thomas H. Ince

Mack Sennett

Louis B. Mayer

Harry Sherman

Nat Levine

U.A.  D. Fairbanks, M. Pickford
D.W. Grifith and C. Chaplan.

Herbert J. Yates

David O. Selznick

# Top 100 Western Movies/T.V. Shows
(Based on entertainment value, story line, and cast of characters.)

1. HOW WEST WAS WON
2. TOMBSTONE
3. DANCES W/ WOLVES
4. OUTLAW JOSEY WALES
5. THE BIG COUNTRY
6. DUEL IN THE SUN
7. LONESOME DOVE
8. QUIGLEY DOWN UNDER
9. SHANE
10 MAN FROM SNOWY RIVER 1&2
11 SILVERADO
12.BUTCH & SUNDANCE
13.LEGENDS OF THE FALL
14 THE WILD BUNCH
15 THE MAGNIFICENT SEVEN
16. MC KENNA'S GOLD
17. WILL PENNY
18. MONTE WALSH
19. WILD ROVERS
20. MAN CALLED HORSE
21. LITTLE BIG MAN
22. DRUMS ALONG THE MOHAWK
23. LAST OF THE MOHICANS
24. RED RIVER
25. JERAMIAH JOHNSON
26. COWBOY (FORD,LEMMON)
27. GERONIMO-WYATT EARP
28. TRUE GRIT
29. UNFORGIVEN
30. BITE THE BULLET
31. BANDELERO
32. THE WAY WEST
33. THE STALKING MOON
34. THE OXBOW INCIDENT

35. THE COWBOYS (J.W.)
36. A BIG HAND FOR THE LITTLE LADY
37. BLOOD ON THE MOON
38. RIVER OF NO RETURN
39. THE SEARCHERS
40. STAGECOACH #2(ALEX CORD)
41. PAINT YOUR WAGON
42. A FISTFUL OF DOLLARS
43 OKLAHOMA
44. RIO BRAVO
45. BLAZING SADDLES
46. CULPEPPER CATTLE CO
47. THE FRISCO KID
48. RIDE THE HIGH COUNTRY
49. CHEYENNE SOCIAL CLUB
50. HALLELUJIA TRAIL
51. VERA CRUZ
52. MANY RIVERS TO CROSS
53. THE KENTUCKIAN
54. CIMARRON ( 1 & 2)
55. THE ROUNDERS
56. STAGECOACH #1 (J.W.)
57. BEND OF RIVER, ETC(J. STEWART)
58. CHISM, BIG JAKE ETC(J.W.).
59. HANG HIGH,  JOE KIDD(C. EASTWOOD)
60. WONDERFUL COUNTRY
61. THE ALAMO (JOHN WAYNE)
62. 2 MULES FOR SISTER SARAH
63. ONE-EYED JACKS
64. NEVADA SMITH
65. THE HUNTING PARTY
66. WHEN LEGENDS DIE
67. IN OLD ARIZONA (CISCO KID)
68. TREASURE OF SIERRA MADRE

69. N.W. MOUNTED POLICE
70. NORTHWEST PASSAGE
71. TOM HORN
72. VILLA RIDES
73. WAGONMASTER
74. TEXAS RANGER
75. UNION PACIFIC
76. WESTERN UNION
77. WATERHOLE  #3
78. THE BRAVADOS
79. WHISPERING SMITH
80. THE SPOILERS
81. THE VIRGINIAN
82. JESSE JAMES
83. THE PLAINSMAN
84. THE WESTERNER
85. THE BIG LAND
86. HEAVENS GATE
87. WINDWALKER
88. STREETS OF LOREDO
89. UNCONQUERD
90. HIGH NOON
91. WESTWARD THE WOMEN
92. SKY FULL OF MOON
93. SCALPHUNTERS
94. JUDGE ROY BEAN
95. TEXAS, & MAN FROM COLO.
    (2 W/G. FORD & WM. HOLDEN)
96. CAT BALLOU
97. TUMBLEWEEDS
98. THE GRAY FOX
99. THE TALL MEN
100. LEGND OF THE
     LONE RANGER

EXAMPLES OF SOME OF THE ABOVE MOVIES ON PAGES 396-407.

## ANY OTHER WESTERN MOVIE FEATURING:

1. JOHN WAYNE
2. CLINT EASTWOOD
3 GARY COOPER
4. GREGORY PECK
5 HENRY FONDA

6. ROBERT MITCHUM
7. GLEN FORD
8. JIMMY STEWART
9. BURT LANCASTER
10. JOEL MCCREA

11. RANDOLPH SCOTT
12. ALAN LADD
13. KIRK DOUGLAS
14. TOM SELLECK
15. SAM ELLIOTT

## TOP WESTERN TELEVISION SHOWS.

1. BONANZA
2. GUNSMOKE
3. MAVERICK
4. CHEYENNE
5. THE VIRGINIAN

6. WAGON TRAIN
7. WANTED: DEAD OR ALIVE
8. HAVE GUN WILL TRAVEL
9. RESTLESS GUN
10. BIG VALLEY

11. WYATT EARP
12. HIGH CHAPARRAL
13. RAWHIDE
14. TALES OF WELLS FARGO
15. THE RIFLEMAN

# Western Movie Directors

1. John Ford - The Iron Horse, Stagecoach, The Searchers, My Darling Clementine, Etc.
2. Budd Boetticher - (Randolph Scott West) Glen Ford (Man From the Alamo) 1950's
3. James Cruze - The Covered Wagon, 1923 Pony Express, 1925.
4. Delmer Daves - Glen Ford (Jubal) 1956 & (Cowboy)1958, Glen Ford, Jack Lemmon.
5. Cecil B.deMille - (Showman Director) Epics, Squaw Man 1913 & The Virginian (both Dustin Farnum) Later, Union Pacific, etc.
6. Henry Hathaway - Versatile Western Director (Zane Grey's w/ Randolph Scott) 1950's. Rawhide, N. to Alaska, Nevada Smith & How the West Was Won, etc.
7. Howard Hawks - John Waynes Red River, 1948 & Rio Bravo, The Big Sky, etc.
8. Joseph Kane - Early Republic, 1930's, Three Musketeers, John Wayne, Gene Autry, etc. Later- The Plainsman, Oh Suzanna, The Vanishing American, etc.
9. Burt Kennedy - Return of Magnificent 7, War Wagon, Rounders. - 1960's.
10. Henry King - Barbara Worth (Gary Cooper) 1926. Jesse James 1939, Bravados 1958.
11. Anthony Mann - Jimmy Stewart films.1950's. Man From Laramie, Winchester '73 etc.
12. George Marshall - Destry Rides Again, The Sheepman (Glen Ford)Texas, 1941.
13. Andrew V. McLaglen (son of Victor) 1950's. Many movies by John Wayne and others.
14. Sam Peckinpah - (Controversial) Ten Years Five westerns-Wild Bunch, Ride High Co.
15. Lesley Selander -1930's Buck Jones,Tim Holt, Hopalong. 1940's Rod Cameron and Johnny Mack Brown, etc.
16. George Sherman - Also from B to A films Wayne and Autry, Don Barry to Big Jake.
17. John Sturges - Magnificent Seven, Last Train to Gun Hill, Hallelujah Trail, The Gunfight at the O.K. Corral, etc. 1950's.
18. King Vidor - Billy the Kid, 1938, Duel in the Sun, 1946 Texas Rangers, Northwest Passage, Man Without A Star.
19. Raoul Walsh - Long Career, like Vidor. Started in D.W. Griffith films. Star until Lost an eye. In Old Arizona, The Big Trail (John Wayne's first noted movie) 1930. Dark Command 1940, The Tall Men 1955.
20. William Wellman - Ox Bow Incident, Buffalo Bill,Yellow Sky, Across theWide Mo.
21. William Wyler - The Westerner(G. Cooper) 1940. Big Country(G.Peck)1959, (3) Godfa.

OTHER DIRECTORS-FEW WESTERNS

22. Arthur Penn - Little Big Man 1970.
23. Martin Ritt - Hud 1963 Paul Newman
24. Robert Aldrich - Four For Texas 1963
25. Edward Dmytryk - Alverez Kelly, Broken Lance, 1954, Spencer Tracy.
26. John Huston - The Misfits,'61, Gable
27. John Wayne - The Alamo 1960, Wayne
28. Fritz Lang - Western Union, 1941,Scott
29. Robert Mulligan - Stalking Moon,'68
30. George Stevens - Shane.50's, Alan Ladd
31. Fred Zinneman - High Noon, Oklahoma
32. Wesley Ruggles - Cimarron '30's, Dix
33. Michael Curtiz - Virginia City, Erroll Flynn, Comancheros, John Wayne
34. Nicholas Ray - Johnny Guitar,Run 4 Cover.
35. Robert Parrish -Wonderful Country(Robert Mitchum)
36. Samuel Fuller- Run of the Arrow, (Rod Steiger)

# The Directors

John Ford

Budd Boetticher

Delmer Daves

Cecil B. DeMille

Henry Hathaway

Howard Hawks

Burt Kennedy

Anthony Mann

George Marshal

Andrew V. McLaglan

Sam Peckinpah

John Sturges

King Vidor

Raoul Walsh

William Wellman

William Wyler

449

# Horses of the Western Movies

1. Gene Autry......................Champion
2. Roy Rogers...........................Trigger
3. William S. Hart.......................Fritz
4. Rex Allen..............................Koko
5. Lone Ranger..........................Silver
6. Buck Jones............................Silver
7. Sunset Carson.......................Silver
8. Hoot Gibson..........................Mutt
9. Fred Thomson...............Silver King
10. Ken Maynard.......................Tarzan
11. Tom Mix (Blue).....................Tony
12. Hopalong Cassidy................Topper
13. Tex Ritter....................White Flash
14. Bob Baker.........................Apache
15. Alan Lane.........................Blackjack
16. Guy Madison....................Buckshot
17. Charles Starrett....................Bullett
18. as Durango Kid....................Raider
19. Tom Tyler...........................Baron
20. Eddie Dean........................Copper
21. Dale Evans....................Buttermilk
22. Duncan Renaldo...................Diablo
23. Leo Carrillo.................Loco(Cisco)
24. John Wayne(early).................Duke
25. Tim Holt...............Duke, Lightning

26. Jack Hoxie.........Dynamite,Scout
27. George O'Brien...................Mike
28. Rod Cameron....................Knight
29. Andy Devine.......................Joker
30. Monte Hale.....................Pardner
31. Johnny Mack Brown...........Rebel
32. Smiley Burnette..................Nellie
33. Kermit Maynard.................Rocky
34. Lash LaRue........................ Rush
35. Jack Holt....................Robin Hood
36. Jay Silverheels.....................Scout
37. Bill Elliott...........................Sunny
38. Jack Perrin.......................Starlight
39. Whip Wilson............Silver Bullet
40. Jimmy Wakley....................Sunset
41. Rocky Lane..............(RR)Thunder
42. Bill Elliott................(RR) Thunder
43. Don Red Barry...............Thunder
44. Fred Harman(Art)............Thunder
45. Joel McCrea.........................Dollar
46. John Wayne(later)................Dollar
47. Jimmy Stewart.......................Pie
48. Jennifer Jones(film).................Dice
49. Charlton Heston................Domino
50. Randolph Scott......................Steel

# Horse Film Stars

Fritz

1. Rex - Silent and "Smoky"
2. Black King'30's after Rex
3. Midnight (in silents)
4. Black Diamond,50's,20yr.
5. Diamond Jet.Versatile 60s
6. Dice(Duel in the Sun) 40s
7. Domino(Big Country) 50s
8. Fury (T.V. Series)
9. Flika &Thunderhead(2)
10. Steel -Star of 40s-50s
11. Mister Ed (T.V.)Alan Lane
12. King Cotton, Lg.Wh.60's
13. Misty (Fat Jones Stables)*
14. Old Baldy(Rearing Horse)
15. Old Fooler(Rounders)
16. Smoky(Cat Ballou)

**\*Randall Ranch and Fat Jones Stables trained and kept movie horses for studios and stars.**

**Champion**

**Trigger**

**Silver**

**Topper**

Tony

Silver

Tarzan

Mutt (Goldie)

Koko

Scout

Rebel

Raider

Dollar

Steel

Blackjack

Diablo

Pie

Pardner

Rush

Ring-Eyed Nellie

Dice

Domino

Smoky

Hidalgo

451

# Family Movie Connections

John Wayne Family

Harry and Olive Carey and Jr.

Wallace

Noah Sr.

Noah Jr.

The Beerys

Like Family

ohn Carradine

*"The Long Riders"*
L.to R. : 3 Carradines as Younger brothers. Keach brothers as James brothers. Quaid bros. as Clel and Ed Miller and the Guest brothers.

Jack, Tim and Jennifer Holt.

Walter, John and Angelica Huston.

The Barrymores

Ethyl, Lionell, John, John Drew and Drew.

Jeannette Nolan.

John and Tim McIntyre.

Tyrone Power Sr. and Jr.

Fred Kohler Jr. and Sr.

Roy Rogers family.

Alan Hale Sr. and Jr.

Charlie Stevens (Geronimo's Grandson)

Louis Jean Heydt
James Millican

# Author's Paintings

2 Paintings by the Author Ken Owens portraying John Wayne's film career.

## Kendall Owens

Author's son's
watercolor paintings.

Original photo of
John Wayne on left
watercolor painting
on the right.

Original photo of
Hopalong Cassidy on
left watercolor painting
on the right.

If you desire an accurate
watercoloer painting of
your kids, grandkids or
celebrities contact :
kendallowens@cox.net

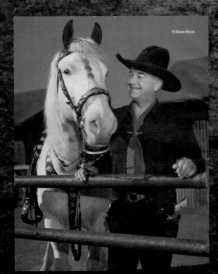

# Closing Remarks

As you can see, this book has no index, but many tables of contents, one at the beginning of the book and another at the beginning of each chapter. There is also no acknowledgments page because the dedication page, the bibliography, and other parts of the book are acknowledgment enough.

This book is intended to show you about 2,000 images of western stars, their directors, their horses, some western history makers, and the western movies themselves. It also helps you to recognize their signatures and gain some idea of what those signatures and autographs are worth.

Over the years, some producers and studio heads have criticized westerns, but the western has prevailed even to this day, as seen by the post-1990s DVDs on page 432.

Various pages in the book can be a challenge for you, to see if you can name those stars not identified in some group or individual photos. They are all identified elsewhere. If you find some, telephone, telegraph, tell-a-friend, but don't tell me. If I missed a favorite star of yours, I apologize.

The western movie has had myself and many others hooked as fans for over 100 years. Now it is your turn. I feel the worst western movie is almost always better than anything else.

Best western wishes. Enjoy!

— **Ken Owens**

# Author's Page

**Educator**

**Entertainer**

**Western Antique Dealer**

**Author/ Artist**

## Ken Owens

Born in northwest Arkansas in 1938, interested in history and archaeology most of his life, Ken also played music through college. He earned a B.A. degree in history at the University of Arkansas, Fayetteville, and an M.S. degree at Oregon College of Education, Monmouth. He taught high school in Arkansas for two years.

Ken then worked twelve years as a teacher, teacher supervisor, and principal for the B. I. A. on the Navajo Indian Reservation in Arizona and New Mexico. Over the years, Ken has been a member of the following archaeological societies: northwest Arkansas; Central States; Tennessee; and San Juan at Farmington, New Mexico.

For the past thirty years to date, Ken has been an Old West and Indian antiques dealer at shows across the western United States.

You can contact Ken at: kokorral@aol.com

## Kalin Owens – Graphic Designer

Kalin was born in Farmington, New Mexico, in 1969. After high school, he completed course work in computer aided drafting at I. T. T. Tech in Phoenix, Arizona, and since has worked as a computer draftsman. Now Kalin lives with his wife, Kristi, and children, Benjamin, Thomas, and Katherine, in northwest Arkansas.

# Bibliography

Cowboy Movies - Norman V. Richards.

Encyclopedia of Western Movies, The - Phil Hardy.

Filming of the West, The - Jon Tuska.

Great Cowboy Stars of Movies and Television, The - Lee O. Miller.

History of Western Movies - Leonard Matthews.

Hollywood Corral - Don Miller.

Hollywood Cowboy Heroes - Screen Greats.

Horses in the Movies - H.F. Hintz.

How the West was Won - Movie Book.

Movie Treasury of the Western Movies, The - Walter C. Clapham.

Owens, Ken - Lifetime collection of over 1000 western movie photos & autographs.

Pictorial History of Westerns, A - Michael Parkinson & Clyde Jeavons.

Saturda;y Evening Post - Movie Book.

Thrill of it All, The - Alan G. Barbour.

Thunder in the Dust - John R, Hamilton.

T.V. Western Book, Official, and T.V. Western Round-Up Book - Neil Summers & Roger M. Crowley.

Complete Films of John Wayne, The - Marc Ricci, Boris and Steve Zhyjemsky.

Duke, The, A Life in Pictures - Rob L. Wagner.

Wayne and the Movies, John, - Allen Eyles.

Wayne, a Tribute, John, - Norm Goldstein and The Associated Press.

Western Films, Heroes, Heavies and Sagebrush - Arthur F. McClure & Ken D. Jones.

George Marshall recieves plaque for 25 years as Western Movie Director.